# Mooting and Advoca

AUSTRALIA
Law Book Co.
Sydney


CANADA and USA
Carswell
Toronto


HONG KONG
Sweet & Maxwell Asia


NEW ZEALAND
Brookers
Auckland


SINGAPORE and MALAYSIA
Sweet & Maxwell Asia
Singapore and Kuala Lumpur

# Mooting and Advocacy Skills

*by*

### DAVID POPE,
*LL.B (Hons.) (Edin.), LL.M (Harvard) of Lincoln's Inn, Barrister,*
*Director of Advocacy, Denton Wilde Sapte LLP*

### DAN HILL,
*MA (Cantab) Head of Practice (Dispute Resolution) and*
*Associate Professor at the College of Law of England and Wales*

THOMSON

SWEET & MAXWELL

Published in 2007 by
Sweet & Maxwell Limited of
100 Avenue Road London NW3 3PF
http://www.sweetandmaxwell.co.uk

Typeset by LBJ Typesetting Ltd,
Kingsclere
Printed in England by Ashford Colour Press, Gosport, Hants

A CIP catalogue record for this book is available from the British Library

ISBN 978-0-421-92470-3

No natural forests were destroyed to make this product, only farmed timber
was used and re-planted.
The Thomson trademark and Star Design are trademarks of Thomson Financial S.A.
used herein under licence.

# Foreword

Good advocacy is an essential tool for practice in the courts of this country. While experience no doubt hones the skills, a basic understanding of what is required, coupled with some confidence in one's own ability to perform, is an essential starting point in an advocate's career. The first court appearance is always a little daunting and particularly the fear that the tribunal may ask a difficult question to which there is no obvious answer (judicial interventions: see chapter 11). By the time the advocate has failed to answer the question, the train of thought has been disrupted and disaster looms.

Mooting, as this excellent book informs the reader, has been around for centuries, but it has never been more important than now, nor more useful as an aid to advocacy training. Happily, mooting is alive and well at our universities through the National Mooting Competition and other informal competitions, in law schools, in the Inns of Court and in all advocacy training. The dreaded video machine is also being used more and more so that no mistake or hesitation goes without notice. That said, the more practice, through mooting and advocacy training, aspiring advocates can obtain, the better equipped they will be to launch their careers. In addition, no C.V. will be complete without some experience of mooting or advocacy training.

This book provides the student with an admirable guide to mooting and advocacy using the case of *Henry Cecil v Charles Dickens* by way of illustration. There are useful hints on preparing for, and conducting, moots, providing advice which is helpful to all advocates starting out on their careers. The message throughout the book is "be prepared". Advice is provided on everything the aspiring advocate needs including what to wear (and what not to wear!), how to stand and dealing with the different forms of address to use to the tribunal.

This book is essential reading for those starting out on their careers as advocates. It will be a useful guide to those who teach advocacy and organise moots as well as those being taught and I thoroughly commend it.

*Christopher Symons Q.C.*

3 Verulam Buildings
Gray's Inn
London

# Preface

The idea to write this book sprang from our involvement in the mooting competition at the College of Law in London. After a number of years of organising it (in Dan's case), giving masterclasses (in David's case) and judging (in both our cases), we had considerable experience of mooting to draw on. David had also been heavily involved in mooting at university, albeit at a time when Margaret Thatcher was still Prime Minister. Surely, we surmised, it could not be too difficult to turn our accumulated knowledge and notes into a student textbook.

How wrong we were. It took us more than a year just to write the proposal to Sweet & Maxwell. Another three years elapsed before we completed the manuscript. This tome was definitely not built in a day.

Since the idea of writing this book first came to us, our aim has been to produce a guide that emphasises the practical. Wherever possible, we have therefore accompanied descriptions of the skills involved in mooting with concrete examples. Many of our examples are based on a typical moot problem that, with a nod to two doyens of legal literature, we have entitled *Henry Cecil v Charles Dickens*. We hope that this practical approach has resulted in a book that will provide genuine assistance to those involved in mooting and lower court advocacy. We also hope that the book manages to convey a sentiment that we both hold dear: mooting is fun.

No writing project of this duration could have survived without the forbearance of a patient and understanding editor. In our case, we were lucky to have just such a person in Nicola Thurlow. Our thanks also go to Richard de-Friend of the College of Law for commenting so perceptively on an early draft of the text, to Leonard Wallace of the Scottish Bar for his invaluable help with a number of points of Scots law and procedure, to Amanda Gray for preparing the posters that we reproduce in the appendices and to Samantha Siddle of Sweet & Maxwell for putting together the marketing material. Finally, we would like to thank our wives, Holly Pope and Susan Short, not only for their unfailing encouragement and support, but also for the umpteen incisive comments that they provided on various drafts of the manuscript.

London                                                        *David Pope*
July 2007                                                      *Dan Hill*

# Contents

# Preparing

## 4 Skeleton arguments

## 5 Notes for oral submissions

## 6 Authorities and bundles

## 7 Practising oral submissions

# Appearing

## 8 Getting your bearings

## 9 Moot court etiquette

## 10 Oral submissions

## 11 Judicial interventions

# Organising

## 12 Organising moots

## Appendices

# 1 Introduction

This book is principally about mooting. It focuses on the practicalities of mooting and on **1–1** organising moots. But the ambit of this book extends beyond the moot courtroom. For in the process of describing how to moot, it provides a toolkit for preparing and delivering persuasive legal arguments. It is therefore intended as a guide not only for those who are involved in mooting competitions, but also for those who are embarking on professional practice.

This opening chapter provides a general overview of mooting by reference to three questions: what is a moot, why should you moot, and where can you moot? The answers to these questions set the scene for the remainder of the book. By way of brief diversion, this chapter ends with a short history of mooting.

The next two sections of the book, entitled "Preparing" and "Appearing", describe the skills that students must develop in order to become effective mooters. Those skills range from conducting legal research and drafting skeleton arguments, to knowing the proper modes of address for moot judges. The final section of the book, entitled "Organising", looks in detail at how to organise mooting competitions.

## What is a moot?

A moot is a competitive mock court hearing. It takes the form of a debate about the legal **1–2** merits of an appeal in a fictitious civil or criminal case. In the United Kingdom, moots are not concerned with the niceties of court procedure and are not mock trials. There are consequently no witnesses and no juries at moots.

Most moots in the United Kingdom, as well as in many Commonwealth jurisdictions, follow a recognised format, which is described in summary below and in far greater detail throughout the rest of this book. Although the primary focus of this book is English law moots, references are made wherever possible to the position in Scotland.

### Participants in a moot

Moots generally involve two teams of two law students, one of whom acts as "leading" or **1–3** "senior" counsel, and the other of whom takes on the mantle of "junior" counsel. The team members normally decide between themselves who will take on which role, although the more experienced mooter, if there is one, will usually be leading/senior counsel.

Both teams present their arguments to a judge or panel of judges. Moot judges are typically law lecturers, postgraduate students or practising lawyers. One team represents the fictitious party that lost in the lower court and is appealing against that decision. The other team represents the fictitious party that won in the lower court and wants that decision to be upheld on appeal. In civil cases, the appealing party is referred to as "the appellant"[1] and the other party as "the respondent". The same nomenclature applies to defendants in criminal appeals, except that the prosecution is always known as "the Crown".

Aside from the mooters and the judge, many moots also feature a moot court clerk. He or she is usually a student who has been roped in by the moot organiser. The court clerk's principal task is to time each mooter's speech, but he or she may also act as a "master of ceremonies", instructing those assembled at the moot to stand when the judge enters the room (customarily with the words "court rise") and then announcing the name of the case once everyone is seated. The court clerk's role may even extend to setting up the moot courtroom and ensuring that the judge has copies of all of the relevant documents.

## Build-up to the moot

1–4    In advance of the moot, usually one or two weeks beforehand, the teams are given identical copies of a written legal problem—the moot problem—and told which party they will represent. The moot problem will, amongst other things, describe the factual background that gave rise to the fictitious proceedings, explain the progress of the case to date, and summarise the decision of the lower court. It will also list the grounds of appeal against the lower court's decision. Moot problems are often based on actual reported cases, but with a number of added twists to ensure that the points that they raise have not already been decided by the courts.

In the period between receiving the problem and the day of the moot, the teams research the legal issues that the problem raises, formulate their arguments, prepare notes to assist them at the moot, and practise delivering their speeches. An advocate's arguments, whether written or oral, are commonly known as "submissions". Some mooting competitions require the teams to serve short skeleton arguments that summarise their submissions in writing. All mooting competitions require the teams to exchange in advance lists of the authorities—the decided cases, textbooks, journal articles and other publications—on which their arguments rely.

## Conduct of the moot

1–5    Moot courtrooms are arranged to resemble real courts. There are consequently designated places for each mooter and for the judge. There is also a seat for the moot court clerk, if there is one, as well as a public gallery where the audience (usually a motley assortment of fellow students and faculty members) can observe the proceedings. A number of law faculties have dedicated moot courtrooms. With their oak-panelled walls and coats of arms above the judges' chairs, these simulated courts sometimes look more authentic than the real thing.

---

[1] In Scotland, a party appealing from the Outer House of the Court of Session to the Inner House is known as "the reclaimer" rather than "the appellant".

Once the moot begins, each mooter speaks in a pre-determined order, presenting his or her arguments and responding to the other side's case. Just as in professional practice, the moot judge has the right (which is almost always exercised) to interrupt the mooters with questions at any point during their speeches. Throughout the proceedings, mooters must observe the requirements of moot court etiquette.

The rules of every mooting competition stipulate the maximum amount of time that the mooters are allowed in which to present their oral submissions (hence the need for a court clerk to time them). Some mooting competitions ignore the time taken to ask and answer questions in computing the maximum period allowed for each mooter's submissions. Others do not. Depending on the competition rules, and whether or not the judge is an interventionist, the oral arguments at moots usually last for between 60 and 90 minutes.

It is a golden rule of mooting that the participants must accept as a given the facts set out in the moot problem, however implausible they may seem and however inconvenient they may be to the arguments that they wish to make. The mooters' submissions must therefore be confined to points of law and, to a lesser extent, policy.

## Conclusion of the moot

Once the mooters have completed their oral submissions, the moot judge gives judgment, **1–6** often after retiring to another room for a few minutes. The judgment consists of two elements: a decision on the law determining which of the fictitious parties has succeeded in the appeal; and a verdict on which team has won the moot.[2] Most judges give judgment in that order, starting with a determination of the points of law that have been argued before announcing the all-important result. Before, or immediately after, announcing the verdict on the moot, most judges briefly address what they regard as the strengths and weaknesses of each mooter's performance (hopefully as tactfully as possible), and offer some words of wisdom on advocacy technique. This can be a useful opportunity for mooters to receive constructive feedback on their performances.

Although judges are often guided in their decisions on the moot by specific criteria set out in the competition rules, the winner of the moot is almost always the team[3] that demonstrates the better advocacy skills and the more comprehensive knowledge of the substantive legal issues. It is accordingly entirely possible—and, indeed, very common—for the winner of the moot to lose on the law.

## Why should you moot?

Mooting is hard work. If taken remotely seriously, it involves many hours of leafing through **1–7** case reports and textbooks, forces the competitors to think deeply about the legal issues raised by the moot problem, and can induce in anyone without nerves of steel stress levels

---

[2] Occasionally, mooting competitions are organised in such a way that the winners of each moot are the two best individual mooters rather than the best team. In these competitions, the judge's verdict identifies the winning individuals.

[3] Or the individuals, if the competition is so structured.

on a par with those occasioned by major examinations. For the very unlucky few, mooting can even result in public humiliation. That experience befell writer and broadcaster Ned Sherrin. Interviewed in *The Times* a few years ago, he described the most embarrassing moment of his life as follows:

> *"I was one of four young barristers who had to argue a mock trial in Gray's Inn. I had divided my brief with my partner, but when he got up to speak he was doing the part that I had prepared. When it came to me the judge gave me a rough time. Suddenly I heard bells ringing and saw a bright purple light—and I fainted."*[4]

Perhaps unsurprisingly after this experience, Mr Sherrin decided against a career at the Bar.

So why moot? Why put yourself through the hard work, the stress and the possibility of keeling over in public? In truth, there are many reasons, some of which are discussed below.

## Mooting makes you think like a lawyer

1–8   In preparing for and appearing at a moot, the participants must do the very things that most practising lawyers do on a daily basis (except charge exorbitant amounts of money for their time). They must quickly absorb a set of facts, identify the relevant legal principles, and apply those principles to the facts. Not only that, but they must also analyse the moot problem from different angles in order to anticipate, and hopefully refute, the arguments that the other side will make. For practitioners, the ability to analyse legal problems in this way is essential if they are to represent their clients' interests effectively.

## Mooting improves your public speaking skills

1–9   For those intent on a career at the Bar or as a solicitor advocate, practice at mooting is plainly invaluable. But presenting and defending a reasoned argument is something that all lawyers should learn to do. Even those who choose to become corporate lawyers, for example, and who will consequently never find themselves representing clients in court, need to be able to make formal presentations to clients and provide internal training to junior members of their departments.

## Mooting is the best way to learn the law

1–10   In order to identify and present persuasive arguments, mooters must obtain a detailed understanding of the legal issues with which the moot problem is concerned. If they are to acquire that understanding, they must hone their research skills beyond the level otherwise required by the legal syllabus. It is not enough, for example, for mooters to read a few select passages from a student textbook and scan the headnotes of a couple of the leading cases. They must read the entirety of a large number of reported decisions, analyse the leading judgments correctly, and work out the *ratio* of each case.

---

[4] *The Times*, 22 July 2003.

Since moots tend to raise topical issues in core subjects such as the law of contract and negligence, there is very often an overlap with examination questions. As a result, it is a common refrain of mooters that they remembered the law covered in a moot so well that they did not have to spend much time revising it for their year-end exams.

## Mooting gives you confidence

Most students come to mooting with very little experience of the law. Understandably, they **1–11** often wonder whether they have what it takes to join the ranks of the legal profession. The sheer similarity of mooting to professional practice gives those who moot an enormous amount of confidence in their abilities as lawyers. And why not? If you are able to stand in front of seasoned law tutors or practitioners and persuade them of the merits of your legal arguments, you know that you can cut the mustard.

## Mooting will help you to find a job

Although there are now greater opportunities than ever for solicitors to appear in court, **1–12** advocacy remains a small and specialised area in terms of the number of practitioners relative to the legal profession as a whole. It is consequently a competitive area to break into. Students wishing to become advocates must therefore demonstrate to interviewers that they are genuinely interested in, and committed to, the life of an advocate. There is no better way for a student to communicate that message than to moot.

The parallels between mooting and real-life advocacy can also give students who are thinking of becoming advocates a good indication of whether that life really is for them. If it is not, far better to find out sooner rather than later. Just ask Ned Sherrin.

## Mooting is fun

Believe it or not, the vast majority of students really enjoy mooting. Like all public speaking, **1–13** it is genuinely exhilarating. A polished performance, whether on the winning or losing side, will provide a sense of achievement and a "buzz" that few other legal (in the broadest sense of the word) activities can match. But mooting is not just about personal highs. It also has a strongly social element, providing an opportunity to get to know your fellow students as well as members of the teaching staff and the legal profession.

# Where can you moot?

The chances are that, if you have managed to find your way to this book, you have already **1–14** located a mooting competition in which to participate. If you are a university student, you probably did not have to search very hard. Most law faculties in the United Kingdom now harbour mooting societies or hold mooting competitions under the auspices of university law societies.

For those of you who are not experiencing the joys of an undergraduate legal education, there are still plenty of places to moot. Many of the institutions in England and Wales that offer the Graduate Diploma in Law (GDL), the Legal Practice Course (LPC) or the Bar Vocational Course (BVC), including the College of Law, organise regular mooting competitions. Each of the Inns of Court[5] also arranges moots for its student members.

In addition to intra-institution moots, there is a host of intervarsity competitions. Some are limited to teams of undergraduates. Others permit postgraduates to compete. There is even a handful of international mooting competitions that offer the opportunity for mooters from this country to pit their skills against their brethren from overseas.

The current contact details of some of the leading intervarsity mooting competitions in the United Kingdom are set out in Appendix I of this book. If you require further information, you will probably find it at *www.mootingnet.org.uk*, which contains a remarkably comprehensive list of national and international mooting competitions.

# A (very) brief history of mooting

**1–15**   The word "moot" appears to derive from an ancient Scandinavian word for a meeting or assembly of people. This derivation suggests that the Vikings may have brought the word to Britain, although it is hard to imagine bands of hairy Norsemen marauding up and down the North Sea coast raping, pillaging and organising mooting competitions.

By whatever means mooting arrived on British shores, it was the mainstay of an English legal education by the late Fifteenth and early Sixteenth centuries. The Inns of Court, which at that time provided both accommodation and legal training to aspiring barristers, held regular moots throughout the academic year. Like their modern-day equivalents, these moots took the form of oral arguments, although they were based on highly complex moot problems that were designed to test the mooters' knowledge of court procedure as well as the law. The most senior members of the Inns, the Masters of the Bench or "benchers", acted as moot judges.

**1–16**   Mooting reached a peak of popularity during the reign of Henry VIII. (One wonders how many English moot problems of the early Sixteenth century featured the law of divorce.) In 1539, for example, one of the earliest legal textbooks to be published in England appeared. It contained an edition of Magna Carta and other ancient statutes as well as "*an Alminacke & a Calendar to know the mootes. Necessarye for all yong studiers of the lawe.*" As the Sixteenth century wore on, however, mooting began a slow and steady decline. A century after Henry VIII's demise in 1547, it had passed from an indispensable element of the English legal curriculum to a voluntary pastime for enthusiastic law students.

Little changed until the late Nineteenth and early Twentieth centuries when mooting societies began to spring up at the Inns of Court and in university law faculties around the country. The popularity of mooting has since grown dramatically, fuelled partly, no doubt, by an increasing emphasis in legal education on teaching practical skills, and by the greater

---

[5] The Inns of Court are ancient unincorporated bodies of lawyers that have the power to call their members to the English Bar. There are four Inns of Court: Lincoln's Inn, Inner Temple, Middle Temple and Gray's Inn.

advocacy opportunities afforded to solicitors in modern-day professional practice. Although it remains a largely extracurricular activity, mooting is returning to the mainstream of legal education. Indeed, in a move that harks back to the halcyon days of Tudor England, some seats of legal learning now teach mooting as a compulsory element of their degree courses. It seems that, once more, mooting is becoming a must for all *yong studiers of the lawe*.

# Preparing

*"Preparation is the be-all of good trial work. Everything else—felicity of expression, improvisational brilliance—is a satellite around the sun. Thorough preparation is that sun."*

Louis Nizer (1902–1994)

# 2 Moot problems

Preparation for a moot begins when you receive the moot problem. You cannot start to **2–1** research the law or to formulate your arguments until you know what the moot is about. The moot problem will tell you. Once you have it, those few paragraphs of text will be ever-present in your life for the days or weeks until the moot takes place.

But what do moot problems look like and how should you go about reading them? These are essentially the questions that this chapter sets out to answer. It also introduces you to the model moot problem of *Cecil v Dickens*, which will supply numerous illustrations throughout the remainder of this book.

## What is a moot problem?

It would be perfectly possible to organise a legal debate along similar lines to a union-style **2–2** debate. The teams might, for example, speak to the motion that *"This House believes that the law of negligence has no place in social situations?"* But that is not the form that moots take. In order to render them more lifelike and, frankly, more interesting, moots revolve around a moot problem. Often as short as a single page and rarely longer than two, the moot problem describes a hypothetical case in narrative form. It also identifies, more or less specifically, the issues of law that the mooters will debate.

## The illustrative moot problem: *Cecil v Dickens*

You will understand far more clearly what a moot problem is if you actually see one. Set out **2–3** in figure 2.1 is therefore a moot problem entitled *Cecil v Dickens*. It is concerned with the law of negligence and is representative of the type of problem that is commonly used for undergraduate and postgraduate mooting competitions. In fact, it has been "road tested" in more than one competitive moot.

The text of *Cecil v Dickens* is not provided simply to show you what a moot problem looks like. *Cecil v Dickens* will be the backdrop for numerous illustrations of mooting skills later in this book and it is accordingly anticipated that you will occasionally wish to remind yourself of what it says. Although *Cecil v Dickens* is an English law moot problem, there is a substantial overlap in the law of negligence in England and Scotland. It is therefore hoped that Scottish mooters will find it both comprehensible and instructive.

## Figure 2.1: *Cecil v Dickens*

2–4

---

IN THE COURT OF APPEAL (CIVIL DIVISION)

HENRY CECIL
-and-
CHARLES DICKENS

Henry Cecil is a self-employed minicab driver trading as "Cecil and Sons". In January 1999, Cecil and Sons bought "Copperfield Cars", a rival minicab business, for £200,000. Prior to the acquisition, Henry commissioned a report from Wickfield's, a local firm of accountants. Wickfield's advised that it had reviewed the accounts of Copperfield Cars for the previous three accounting periods and that, in view of Copperfield Cars' net profits and assets, the purchase price was reasonable.

In late 2001, it became obvious to Henry that the business of Copperfield Cars was loss-making and that its previous owners had massively overstated its profits and assets. Henry decided to ask his old school friend Charles Dickens for advice. Charles is and was a qualified solicitor practising as "Dickens and Son". In January 2002, Henry met Charles for a drink in a local pub after work, handed him the report written by Wickfield's, and asked Charles what he could do to obtain compensation for the incorrect advice that Wickfield's had given him. Charles listened to Henry's story, took some notes and read through the report. He then said words to the following effect:

> "Henry, old friend, litigation is not my area of expertise as I specialise in conveyancing, but it is my preliminary view that you have an arguable claim against Wickfield's. Litigation is a risky and expensive business, however, and I suggest that you think carefully about whether or not you wish to sue Wickfield's. If you decide to take matters forward, you should consult a law firm called Barkis & Traddles, which specialises in litigation."

Henry developed depression a few months after speaking to Charles. He did not contact Barkis & Traddles until the middle of 2005, when he was told that it was no longer possible for him to sue Wickfield's because the relevant six-year limitation period had expired.

Henry subsequently issued proceedings against Charles for negligently failing to advise him that the limitation period would apply to his potential claim against Wickfield's. At first instance, Mr Justice Steerforth sitting in the Queen's Bench Division of the High Court of Justice found in Henry's favour.

Mr Justice Steerforth made the following findings:

1. Despite the social relationship between them, Charles owed a duty of care in negligence to Henry to avoid causing pure economic loss.

2. Charles breached that duty by not making clear to Henry that a limitation period of six years from the date of acquisition of Copperfield Cars applied to the potential claim against Wickfield's.

3. Had Charles made it clear to Henry that a limitation period applied to the potential claim, Henry would have sought legal advice from Barkis & Traddles before the expiry of the limitation period.

4. Had Henry sued Wickfield's before the limitation period expired, he would have recovered £100,000. This was accordingly the sum to which Henry was entitled in damages from Charles.

Charles now appeals to the Court of Appeal on the following grounds:

1. No duty of care arose in negligence.

2. If, contrary to the first ground of appeal, a duty of care did arise, he did not breach it.

---

# The anatomy of moot problems

The problem of *Cecil v Dickens* follows a fairly standard format. You should therefore find **2–5** that, like *Cecil v Dickens*, most of the moot problems with which you grapple include the following elements, typically in the following order:

- **Identity of the moot court**
  The moot problem should identify, often in the heading, the court in which the moot is going to take place. In most English law moots, the moot court is the Court of Appeal or the House of Lords. Scots law moots tend to take place in the Inner House of the Court of Session or (for criminal law moots) the High Court of Justiciary. As you can see from its heading, *Cecil v Dickens* is a Court of Appeal (Civil Division) case.

- **Background facts**
  The bulk of the moot problem is usually given over to reciting the factual background. The facts may be encapsulated in one or two paragraphs or they may run to a page or more. In *Cecil v Dickens*, they fill the first three paragraphs (down to "*. . . because the relevant six-year limitation period had expired*").

- **Procedural history**
  Most moot problems include a short explanation of the route that the fictitious case took before it reached the moot court. In an English contract law moot problem, for example, the case might pass from a trial before a judge of the High Court, to an appeal before the Court of Appeal (Civil Division), before finding its way to the House of Lords. A Scottish contract law moot problem might feature a case that started life in the Sheriff Court before being appealed to the Inner House of the Court of Session. The procedural history of *Cecil v Dickens* is set out in the fourth paragraph of the problem (beginning "*Henry subsequently issued proceedings . . .*").

- **Findings of the lower court**
  Moot problems almost always contain a synopsis of the lower court's decision. The summary may be short or it may descend to considerable detail. The problem in *Cecil v Dickens* sets out four findings that Mr Justice Steerforth made at first instance.

- **Grounds of appeal**
  Moot problems usually end by listing the grounds of appeal. These are the bases on which the decision of the lower court is being challenged in the moot court. Most moot problems contain at least two grounds of appeal.

# How to read moot problems

Reading the text of *Cecil v Dickens* is unlikely to have given you heart palpitations. When **2–6** you are actually competing in a moot, however, the experience of reading a moot problem for the first time is rather different. The heart rate soars, the eyes pass too quickly over the words, and the mind flits repeatedly between a state of calm comprehension and a fever of rising panic. Anyone afflicted by this unfortunate condition (and that includes most normal human beings) is probably best advised to succumb to it on first reading. Skim read the problem from start to finish. If nothing else, a quick run through should reassure you that the problem contains nothing wholly alien and incomprehensible.

Once your pulse is near normal and your brain has returned to its natural equilibrium, it is time to embark on the serious business of reading the moot problem critically. You should go through it slowly at least two or three times. Ensure that you understand what each sentence means before you move on to the next. If the facts are complicated, reduce them to a comprehensible format as you go along. If, for example, the problem involves a number of inter-related companies, draw a diagram of the group structure so that you can see how it fits together. Similarly, if the problem refers to events that took place on a number of different dates, jot down a short chronology so that you are clear about the order in which they occurred.

As you read the moot problem, all sorts of thoughts may run through your head. You may well be vaguely familiar with the areas of law involved and may consequently remember some of the general principles or recall the names of one or two of the leading cases. You may also find yourself constructing arguments and compiling lists of questions to research. Make notes as you go along. Sometimes, the points that you spot at this very early stage are amongst the most insightful. You do not want to forget them.

Before you get too carried away, however, make sure that you have answered the four questions discussed below.

## Which party do you represent?

2–7    When you receive the moot problem, you should be told which party you represent. You must ensure that you know which party is which. You might think that this will be blindingly obvious, but sometimes it is not. The headings of most moot problems identify the parties in the format "claimant/pursuer v defendant/defender". That is true of *Cecil v Dickens*, in which Mr Cecil is the claimant and Mr Dickens is the defendant. Yet Mr Cecil's claim succeeded before the High Court judge and it is Mr Dickens who is appealing against that decision to the Court of Appeal. Mr Dickens is therefore the appellant in the moot and Mr Cecil is the respondent. If you were told that you were acting for the appellant, you would accordingly be representing Mr Dickens, even though his name appears second in the title of the problem.

If you are in any doubt about which party you represent, check with the moot organiser. It is far better to ask what might seem like a silly question than to join the ranks of mooters— and there are many out there—who have started to research a problem on behalf of the wrong party.

## What is the relevance of each of the facts?

2–8    As you read through the section of the moot problem that describes the factual background, you should ask yourself repeatedly whether you understand the significance of each of the given facts. Although some moot problem authors are more prone than others to embellishing their work with irrelevant background information, most of the facts in a well drafted moot problem will be helpful to one or other of the parties. They should consequently give you plenty of clues for arguments that you or your opponents might run.

You should remember that the facts of a moot problem are sacrosanct. They may be ludicrously far-fetched and unhelpful to your case, but you are stuck with them. You cannot therefore invite the judge to change them or to make additional factual findings. For example, Mr Cecil's case in *Cecil v Dickens* would be considerably strengthened if he had paid Mr Dickens for the advice that he received. But there is no mention of payment in the moot problem and the participants must therefore assume that none was made. The mooters representing Mr Cecil could not therefore invite the judge at the moot to find that Mr Dickens was paid, even in the form of a couple of pints.

## On what basis did the lower court make its decision?

The summary of the lower court's decision will often include important clues about the **2–9** arguments that you might make at the moot. Some moot problems even refer to the authorities on which the lower court judge relied. They will then provide a starting point for your legal research. Even if you are not that lucky, the lower court's decision can be of considerable assistance. In *Cecil v Dickens*, for example, the third and fourth findings of the trial judge established that Mr Dickens's breach of duty caused him to lose the sum of £100,000. Since Mr Dickens is not appealing against either of these findings, it will be apparent that the moot is not concerned with issues of causation and loss.

## What are the grounds of appeal?

You should read the grounds of appeal with particular care. For just as in appeals before **2–10** real life courts, mooters are usually confined to arguing in support of or against the specified grounds of appeal.

Thus, in *Cecil v Dickens*, the first ground of appeal states that "*No duty of care arose in negligence*". The submissions on this ground of appeal must therefore be directed to the circumstances in which duties of care arise in negligence. If you were acting for Mr Cecil, you could not argue, for example, that there was a contract between him and Mr Dickens under which the latter is liable.

# Discussing the moot problem with your team-mate

If you are mooting as part of a team, you should discuss the moot problem with your partner **2–11** shortly after you receive it. There are two principal reasons for this. The first is that a conversation with your team-mate at this early stage will help you to identify the relevant issues. Your mooting partner may have spotted points that you did not and vice versa. Some of those points may be good, others not so. By debating them, you should produce some useful initial ideas and prevent a few diversionary hares from running. Your discussion should include a consideration of the overall merits of the moot problem. Do you or your opponents have the better of it? What are your weaknesses? What are theirs?

The second reason for having an early discussion about the moot problem is that you can use it as an opportunity to work out how best to divide the legal research between you.

Come the moot, you will need to be reasonably conversant with each other's submissions just in case the judge asks one of you a question that the other was going to cover. It is nonetheless unlikely to be a sensible use of time for both of you to research all of the same ground in detail. Very often, the moot problem itself will present a clear way of splitting the work. In *Cecil v Dickens*, for example, there are (conveniently) two grounds of appeal. Since the second ground of appeal is dependent on the first (if there is no duty of care, it cannot have been breached), the obvious division of labour is for the team member who will speak first to take the first ground of appeal and for the other team member to take the second ground of appeal. The former will then research duty of care, while the latter researches standards of care and breach.

If the moot problem does not present a well-defined division of labour, it may be necessary for you and your team-mate to begin your researches independently. This approach should not result in too much duplication if it is confined to the early stages of research. The position should be kept constantly under review, however. As and when an appropriate allocation of work becomes apparent, the research should be divided up along those lines.

# When you have the weaker case

**2–12** However well crafted the moot problem may be, the legal merits will always favour one side more than the other. For example, the (beautifully crafted) problem of *Cecil v Dickens* favours the appellant, Mr Dickens. As the law of England currently stands, a judge presiding over a moot employing this problem should therefore decide to uphold the appeal when giving judgment on the law.

There may well be times when you read a moot problem and form the view that the merits are against you. But even if you are right, you should remember that the weakness of your legal case is not a bar to you winning the moot. On the contrary, being on the weaker side may even provide a better opportunity to showcase your advocacy skills than having the stronger case because you will have to come up with more creative arguments. For this reason, many seasoned mooters actually prefer to be on the wrong side of the legal merits.

# Summary

**2–13** The moot problem not only sets the scene for the moot, it defines the legal issues with which the moot is concerned and delimits the arguments that the mooters may advance. It is therefore essential that you read it thoroughly and analytically before you launch into your research.

This chapter has discussed moot problems in detail. In particular, it has:

- Identified each of the important elements of a typical moot problem.

- Described how to read moot problems critically.

- Recommended that you discuss the moot problem with your team-mate at an early stage.

- Explained that having the weaker legal case does not mean that you will lose the moot.

# 3 Legal research

**3-1** If your experience of courtroom advocacy is limited to watching *Judge John Deed*, you could be forgiven for thinking that winning a legal argument is all about grandstanding in court. Perhaps it should come as no surprise that television programmes give this impression. After all, it makes for considerably more compelling viewing if a glamorous advocate is eloquently holding forth to the judge rather than perspiring feverishly in the law library, surrounded by pads of paper, law reports and handfuls of "post-it" notes. This media-generated impression is misleading, however. For as any practising advocate will tell you, it is the "hard yards" spent researching the case and constructing arguments that underpin success at trial. Precisely the same principle applies in mooting.

This chapter examines the skills required to conduct research for moots.[1] Many of those skills are employed every day by advocates preparing for court hearings. The chapter begins by discussing the primary objective of research—to formulate persuasive arguments. It then describes the research process, separating it into four phases. After looking at a worked example using the illustrative case of *Cecil v Dickens*, the chapter ends with a short description of the principal sources of research material.

## The ultimate objective: persuasive arguments

**3-2** In a broad sense, the object of your research is to understand each of the legal issues that the moot problem raises. And you need to understand them well; better, in fact, than most areas of the law that you will come across in the course of your undergraduate legal studies. Unless one of your tutors is a die-hard adherent to the Socratic method of teaching, there will certainly be precious few subjects on the legal curriculum about which you will have to give a speech and answer questions in front of an audience.

But a detailed knowledge of the relevant law is not enough to enable you to moot. A moot is a debate about the law and you will be taking one side or the other in that debate. The ultimate objective of your research is therefore to furnish you with the arguments that you will present in your oral submissions and in any skeleton argument that you draft. Those arguments must cover both your positive and negative cases. Your positive case comprises the reasons why you say that the fictitious party you represent should succeed on the law. If

---

[1] This chapter is not, however, a comprehensive guide to conducting legal research. If you need broader assistance with your research skills, you might consult the sister text to this book, *Knowles and Thomas, Effective Legal Research* (2006).

you are acting for the appellant (or the reclaimer in certain Scottish moots), your positive case is therefore the arguments that support each ground of appeal. If you are representing the respondent, by contrast, your positive case is the arguments that demonstrate why each ground of appeal should fail. Whichever party you represent, your negative case is made up of the reasons why you assert that the opposing party's submissions should fail.

Whether part of your positive or negative case, each of your arguments should help to persuade the judge that your team should win the moot. But what makes an argument persuasive and how do you construct persuasive arguments for moots? These are the questions that the next few pages set out to answer.

# The nature of persuasive arguments

The Ancient Greeks (at least, some of them) were fascinated by the persuasive impact that **3–3** particular modes of writing and speaking had on an audience. They even developed a complex field of study known as rhetoric that sought to explain the phenomenon. According to Aristotle, amongst others, persuasion is achieved by using the following three rhetorical "appeals":

- *ethos*, by which the orator seeks to persuade the audience by establishing his own credibility;

- *pathos*, by which the orator appeals to the audience's emotions; and

- *logos*, by which the orator appeals to the audience's reason.

As a man of reason, Aristotle wanted people to be persuaded by *logos* alone. He recognised, however, that there are certain weaknesses in mankind's make-up that render us susceptible to the baser appeals. He therefore advised orators to employ those appeals in addition to *logos* if they wanted to sway an audience. Aristotle would doubtless have approved of mooting because neither *ethos* nor *pathos* has any part to play in persuading a moot judge. *Ethos* is certainly not much use to mooters, who are invariably students with little experience of the law and who therefore lack much in the way of legal credibility. You will not strengthen your argument, for example, if you tell the moot judge how well you did in your last contract law exam. Nor is *pathos* likely to advance a mooter's argument. Whilst some trial lawyers might employ emotional tactics to influence juries, you will not impress a moot judge by declaiming that the fictitious party represented by your opponents is "*a bounder and a cad*" who deserves no sympathy from the court.

In mooting, therefore, a persuasive argument is based on *logos* or logical reasoning. The **3–4** classical forms of logical reasoning are inductive and deductive reasoning. Inductive reasoning involves drawing a conclusion from evidence. It is regularly used in the law courts. For instance, in a murder trial, prosecuting counsel might refer to evidence that the accused was seen in the vicinity of the crime at about the time it was committed and to DNA evidence showing that there were specks of the victim's blood on one of the accused's shirts. Prosecuting counsel might then invite the jury to conclude from this evidence that the accused was the killer. This form of reasoning tends not to feature heavily in moots, however, because all of the relevant facts are provided by the moot problem and are not open for debate. The technique on which mooters must concentrate if they are to build persuasive arguments is therefore deductive, or syllogistic, reasoning.

# Using deductive reasoning

**3–5**  Deductive reasoning involves applying a general rule (the major premise) to a specific situation (the minor premise) in order to reach a conclusion. For example, the following argument employs deductive reasoning:

**Major premise**    All mooters are law students.

**Minor premise**    Sally is a mooter.

**Conclusion**       Therefore Sally is a law student.

In legal argument, deductive reasoning is generally used to establish links between principles of law and the facts of the particular case so as to arrive at a legal conclusion. In systems of law based on precedent (as both the English and Scottish legal systems are), legal principles are derived from recognised "authorities". These authorities come in a "pecking order". The most important for English law purposes are cases decided by the English courts. Lesser forms of authority include, in broadly descending order of influence, leading practitioner textbooks, decided cases from other jurisdictions with similar legal systems,[2] articles published in respected journals and periodicals and, occasionally, student textbooks.[3] In Scotland, the range of authorities is much the same,[4] except that those of greatest value are decisions of the Scottish courts and the institutional writers provide an additional form of authority that has no equivalent in England.

**3–6**    In both England and Scotland, the basic building blocks of a legal argument founded on deductive reasoning are therefore as follows:

**Major premise**    The relevant legal principle, as derived from appropriate authority.

**Minor premise**    The facts of the case at hand.

**Conclusion**       The legal finding that the judge should make.

You will see when you read reported cases that many judges follow these three steps remarkably closely when they give judgment. They often begin their speeches by reviewing the relevant authorities in order to discern the applicable principle of law (the major premise). They then "apply" that principle to the facts of the cases before them (the minor premise) in order to reach their conclusions.

The deductive reasoning model described above will serve as a basis for both your positive and negative cases at a moot. In order to build a positive argument, you must search the relevant authorities for principles of law that, when applied to the critical facts of the moot problem, lead inexorably to the conclusion that you wish the judge to reach. In order to build a negative argument, you must attack the major and minor premises of your opponents' argument. You must, in other words, look for ways to dispute the legal principles

---

[2] The most authoritative jurisdictions for English law purposes are Australia, New Zealand, the United States, Canada and (for contract and tort in particular) Scotland.

[3] One student textbook that makes relatively frequent appearances in the law reports is *Atiyah's Introduction to the Law of Contract*, 6th ed (2006). An earlier edition of the work was referred to, for example, in *Shogun Finance Ltd v Hudson* [2003] UKHL 62; [2004] 1 AC 919, 954.

[4] The jurisdictions with similar systems of law obviously differ from England, however. The Scots law mooter may glean assistance, for example, from the jurisprudence of the South African courts. That learning would be of little help to an English mooter.

that your opponents have drawn from their authorities and argue that those principles, even if valid, do not apply to the facts of the moot problem. If you can do this, you will break the logical thread of your opponents' argument and render its conclusion invalid.

## Overview of the research process

There is no one way to conduct research for any given moot problem. Different people **3–7** manage it equally successfully in different ways. Nonetheless, it is possible to sketch out a basic model for carrying out research for moots. The model comprises the following four phases:

- **Phase 1: understanding the legal context**
  During this phase, which follows a careful reading of the moot problem,[5] you obtain an understanding of the relevant legal backdrop. This is a relatively short, but important, step in the research process.

- **Phase 2: conducting detailed research**
  Phase 2 is when you carry out your in-depth research into each of the grounds of appeal set out in the moot problem. It is usually the longest phase of the research process.

- **Phase 3: finalising arguments and authorities**
  This phase covers the period before you serve your list of authorities and draft any skeleton argument. During this phase, you finalise the arguments that make up your positive case and select the authorities that your team will cite at the moot.

- **Phase 4: refuting your opponents' case**
  The final phase begins when you receive your opponents' list of authorities and skeleton argument (if any). It lasts until the moot. Most of this phase is spent coming up with ways to defeat your opponents' arguments.

No claim is made here that each of these phases can or should form a distinct, hermetically-sealed component of the research process. On the contrary, there will inevitably be significant overlaps between them. Nonetheless, each phase is considered separately below.

## Phase 1: understanding the legal context

It is essential that, from the very beginning of the research process, you understand the **3–8** overarching principles that govern the areas of law with which the moot problem is concerned. If you appreciate the legal context, you will find it far easier to read and make

---

[5] Chapter 2 explains how to read moot problems with care.

the most of the authorities that you come across during your in-depth research. The benefits of a "helicopter view" go further than that, however. Moot problems, by definition, raise unresolved legal issues. In order to reach decisions on those issues, moot judges are usually forced to fall back on first principles. The arguments that you develop must be consistent with those principles. You therefore need to know what they are.

In theory, you could obtain your overview from any number of sources. However, the best place is usually the leading practitioner textbook in the relevant field of law.[6] Practitioner textbooks are ideally suited to this purpose. They focus on "black letter" law, describing the law as it is rather than how it ought to be. They are also accurate, detailed and up-to-date.

If you are unable to lay your hands on the relevant practitioner text, you have two main options. The first is to read the relevant pages of a good student textbook. When compared to practitioner textbooks, student texts are more discursive and less detail-oriented, and they tend to be updated less frequently. You should therefore ensure that any you read was published recently. On the credit side of the ledger, however, student textbooks are likely to be more readily available to mooters because law libraries often stock multiple copies and many students possess copies themselves. In addition, the layout and writing styles of student texts are more accessible than those of practitioner textbooks, and mooters may accordingly find them easier to use.

Your second option is to read the relevant paragraphs of *Halsbury's Laws of England* (for an English law moot) or *The Law of Scotland: Stair Memorial Encyclopaedia* (for a Scots law moot). Neither publication descends to the detail of most practitioner, or even student, textbooks, but both should offer accurate and up-to-date summaries of the guiding legal principles.

3–9        Whichever source you plunder for your understanding of the legal context, you will inevitably come across references to potentially important authorities. You should start to compile a running list of these authorities for use later in the research process. This list will help to ensure that you do not overlook a critical case or text.

Although obtaining an understanding of the context is a vital part of the research process, you are likely to find that it becomes increasingly abbreviated as your legal experience grows. As a wet-behind-the-ears undergraduate preparing for your first moot, you may be completely unfamiliar with an area of law that arises in a moot problem. This phase of the research process will then take up a significant amount of time. By contrast, as a seasoned postgraduate student studying for your vocational exams, you should have a decent grasp of most of the topics that habitually crop up in moots. This phase may then involve little more than reading a few pages of a tried and trusted textbook, and jotting down a handful of references to authority.

## Phase 2: conducting detailed research

3–10      Once you have an overview of the law under your belt, you can start your detailed research. This phase of the research process is essentially a hunt for the authorities that contain the relevant legal principles. It involves three broad elements: identifying potentially relevant

---

[6] Tables 3.5 and 3.6 list some of the leading English and Scots law practitioner textbooks in a number of key disciplines.

authorities; deciding which are sufficiently important to read; and reading those that you consider merit the attention.

## How to identify relevant authorities

You will find potentially relevant authorities by scouring the sources available to you. The **3–11** principal sources of authorities are described at the end of this chapter. They include case reports, textbooks and journal articles. You will probably search through most of them online, although you will still have to refer to plenty of printed material. Relatively few legal textbooks have yet made it into electronic form, for example, so you will have to read them in hard copy. Whenever you come across a reference to an authority of potential interest, you should add it to the running list that you started to compile during the first phase of your research.

You may well find that the process of tracking down authorities resembles an investigation. A footnote in a textbook may lead you to a reported decision that, in turn, refers to another, more helpful, case. You may even come to feel a little like a private detective, hunting high and low for authorities and following up leads with all of the persistence of a latter-day Hercule Poirot.

## How to decide which authorities to read

In the course of your research for a moot, your running list of potentially relevant **3–12** authorities might grow to 50 or more. Most of them will be case reports. A few of these cases will immediately stand out as particularly significant and you will probably read them the moment that you discover them. Since you are unlikely to have sufficient time to read every one of the remaining cases, you will have to develop a system of triage for isolating those that you should read from those that you can safely ignore.

Your ability to separate the wheat from the chaff will improve with experience. But what if you lack that experience? Set out below are four pointers to assist you in eliminating cases of tangential relevance:

- **Concentrate on the cases that crop up most often**
  If you find that a particular case is mentioned time and again, it is probably one of the more important and therefore worth devoting careful attention to.

- **Make full use of the headnote**
  Almost all reported cases, even those accessed online, include a headnote that briefly summarises the facts, the procedural history and the findings of the court. The headnote should therefore provide you with a good indication of whether the case is relevant for your purposes. If that indication is clearly negative, it makes little sense to read through the entire report.

- **Read the most recent decision first**
  If you find a number of cases that address a particular legal issue, read the most recently decided first. It may summarise the earlier cases for you and save you the trouble of reading them. On the other hand, it may refer to cases that are more "on point" and therefore of potentially greater use to you. You can then make a beeline for them.

- **Do not read the first instance decision if the case went to appeal**
  When the lower court and appeal court decisions of a particular case are both reported, you can generally confine yourself to reading the latter. Some series of law reports helpfully reprint the speeches of both the lower and appeal courts next to each other. If the different judgments in a single set of proceedings are reported separately, however, you should ensure that you are reading the higher court decision. It is a sobering experience to wade through a seemingly significant judgment only to find that it was subsequently overturned on appeal.

## How to read authorities

**3–13**   Once you have identified the most important authorities, you need to read them. Thoroughly. Case reports, in particular, require careful attention. If you fail to read an important decided case from beginning to end, you may miss some useful material such as a helpful quote or case reference. Worse than that, you may pick up the wrong end of the stick: in your haste, you might misunderstand a critical part of the leading judgment and believe it to support your case when it goes against you; or you might read a dissenting or differing judgment and mistakenly believe it to represent the views of the majority of the court. These sorts of mistakes can land you in a lot of hot water, particularly if the realisation that you have misread a case only dawns on you at the moot.

**3–14**   As you read through authorities, you should be looking to extract from them material that will help to bolster the arguments that you have already thought of and to identify further, possibly more persuasive, arguments. That task is usually pretty straightforward when you are reading textbooks and articles because the authors will articulate their points in an argumentative way. Drawing material from decided cases can be more complicated. When reading them, you should have your eyes peeled, in particular, for the following:

- **Helpful statements of legal principle**
  Top of your wish list are clear statements of the law that will support your case. What you want is that core sentence or two in which the judge explains what the law is. You will quickly develop a facility for spotting these passages. You must ensure, however, that the helpful excerpt is of general application and is not expressly limited to the facts of the particular case.

- **The judge's reasoning**
  You want to work out how the judge reached the conclusion that he did. Judges usually explain their thought processes before setting out their conclusions. You may be able to apply the same chain of reasoning at the moot.

- **The arguments of counsel**
  Judges often refer in their judgments to the arguments that counsel advanced before them. Some series of law reports summarise counsel's principal submissions at the beginning of each case report. This can be fertile ground for mooters because you can often adapt (or even adopt) counsel's arguments for your own purposes.

# Phase 3: finalising arguments and authorities

Throughout the research process, you ought to be thinking about possible arguments. **3–15** During the early phases of your research, you should concentrate on your positive case. You should, of course, give *some* thought to identifying the thrust of the case that your opponents are likely to make and to considering how you will meet it. If you do so, you will be better placed to refute your opponents' case in detail when you exchange lists of authorities and skeleton arguments (if required). Generally speaking, however, it is unwise to focus too heavily on your negative case until you exchange with the other side because your efforts will be wasted if your opponents take a different tack from the one you were expecting.

As the moot draws nearer, you must decide on the arguments that will make up your positive case and fine-tune them. If you have to serve a skeleton argument in advance of the moot, you will need to settle on the points that appear in it.[7] Even if you do not, you will have to work out which authorities to cite at the moot; since those authorities will support your arguments, you need to know which arguments you will be running.

Most mooting competitions limit the number of authorities that each team can cite, **3–16** sometimes to as few as three. Even if you are free from such a restriction, there is bound to be a time limit on your oral submissions. It will act as an effective constraint on the number of authorities that your team cites because you will simply have insufficient time in which to take the judge through more than a limited selection.

There will usually be a few "automatic picks" amongst the authorities that you cite. These will be the authorities that are fundamental to the arguments that you will run. Often, however, you will also be faced with an array of potentially helpful, but not critical, authorities. The next few pages offer some pointers for choosing which to cite.

## Select the most weighty authorities

As a general rule, you should choose the authorities that carry the greatest legal weight. **3–17** The three factors described below largely determine weight in this sense, the first two being by far the most important.

### *Type of authority*

When you are choosing between different types of authority (i.e., case reports, practitioner textbooks, journal articles, etc.), you should select as many as possible from the upper echelons of the "pecking order" referred to earlier in this chapter. Most, if not all, of the authorities on your list should consequently be decided cases from the higher courts. There may be exceptions, however. For example, when the principles of a particular area of the law are not set out in a single case, but are scattered across a number, you may be better off citing a respected practitioner textbook that summarises the relevant law rather than one reported decision that can only give a partial picture. The moot judge may ask you to justify your choice of authority, but will probably view favourably your explanation that you wanted to save time and were constrained in the number of authorities that you could cite.

---

[7] Chapter 4 looks in detail at drafting skeleton arguments.

*Level of court*

When you are choosing between different reported cases, you should usually base your
selection on where the courts that handed down the decisions appear in the judicial
hierarchy: the more senior the court, the greater the weight that is attached to its decisions.
The court hierarchy in England and Wales is shown, in simplistic terms, in figure 3.1.
Scotland's court structure is rather different and is illustrated, also simplistically, in figure
3.2. As many as possible of the case reports that make it onto your list of authorities should
inhabit the higher reaches of these diagrams.

## Figure 3.1: Hierarchy of courts in England and Wales

**3–18**

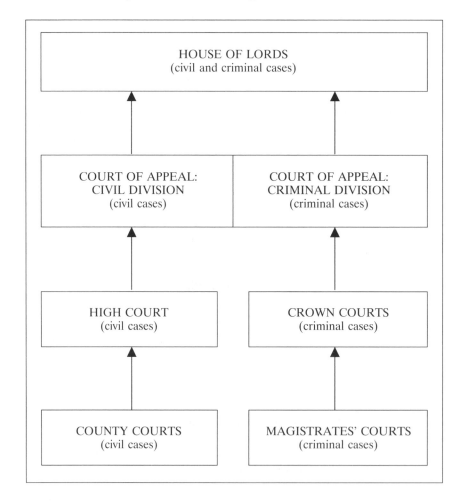

## Figure 3.2: Hierarchy of courts in Scotland

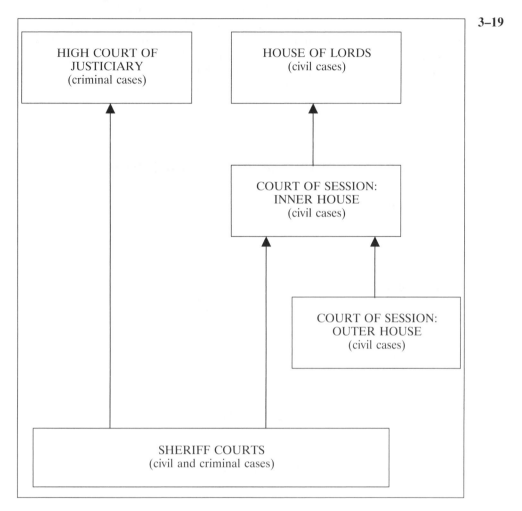

**3–19**

*Reputation of the judge*

A further factor to bear in mind when considering the weight attributed to reported cases is the esteem in which the judges who decided them are held. Although this is not a point worth making a meal of, the fact that a judge is particularly well respected can lend additional weight to his judgments. This is something of a minefield for students new to the law who have little familiarity with legal history, but some names are likely to stand out even at a relatively early stage of your legal studies. Lord Atkin (he of *Donoghue v Stevenson* fame) in the field of negligence is an obvious example.

## Select the most recently decided cases

Where you find yourself with two or more reported cases of roughly equivalent legal weight, **3–20** you should generally cite the most modern decision. You might even cite a recent case in preference to an earlier decision made by a court higher up the judicial hierarchy if it contains a helpful summary of the present state of the law or of the way in which the law has developed. The modern tendency of judges to produce lengthy judgments means that you are quite often presented in a single speech not only with a helpful recitation of the relevant legal principles, but with a smörgåsbord of excerpts from the leading authorities. By citing a case such as this, you can take the moot judge to the most important passages in a number of other cases. However, there are limits to how far you can take this approach without infringing the rules of most mooting competitions. In particular, you cannot normally cite a case that refers to other authorities and then seek to introduce material about those other authorities that does not appear in the case that you have cited.

## Be wary of dissenting or differing judgments

**3–21**    As a general rule, you should only cite a case in order to rely on the views expressed by the majority of the court. That is not to say that you should never rely on a minority judgment. The dissenting judge may, for example, have disagreed only on the facts, his reasoning on the law having been accepted by the remainder of the court. You may then safely use that reasoning to bolster your case. You might also cite a minority judgment of a particularly distinguished member of the judiciary whose dissenting view has subsequently been held to represent the law. But you need to be careful, particularly if the speeches of the majority of the court are unhelpful to your case and can consequently be relied on by your opponents. For similar reasons, you must beware of relying on the words of judges who, although in the majority in upholding or rejecting an appeal, reached their decisions for different reasons from the remainder of the tribunal.

## Do not cite unhelpful authorities

**3–22**    Mooters acting on behalf of appellants are particularly prone to the affliction of citing authorities that are against them. Their rationale is usually that, because they will be addressing the moot court first, they can "rubbish" the authority before their opponents get to their feet.

Citing authorities in this way is almost always a mistake. If the authority is genuinely helpful to your opponents, they will probably cite it themselves, in which case you can address it when you refute their arguments during your oral submissions. If your opponents do not cite the authority and you do, you will needlessly present them with additional ammunition.

## Less is sometimes more

**3–23**    Citing more authorities does not guarantee a better argument. If you are satisfied that you already have enough authorities of sufficient weight to make good the arguments that you intend to advance at the moot, there is nothing to be gained from citing further, makeweight authorities simply because you are allowed to. Nor should you indulge in the tiresome sport of deliberately citing off beam (and usually lengthy) authorities in the hope of sending your opponents on a wild-goose chase. Even if your opponents take the bait, the judge or the moot organiser will probably spot the attempted deception. They will not be impressed.

# Phase 4: refuting your opponents' case

The final phase of the research process begins when you receive your opponents' list of **3–24** authorities and any skeleton argument that they have drafted, and lasts until the start of the moot. During this period, the primary focus of your research is usually your negative case, that is to say the refutation of the other side's arguments.[8] If your opponents have served a skeleton, it should tell you explicitly what those arguments will be. Even if you only see a list of your opponents' authorities, however, you should be able to work out quite accurately what the other side will say. Gleaning the other side's arguments and refuting them effectively will require you to read carefully each of the authorities on which your opponents rely.

You should analyse your opponents' case with the same logical rigour that you brought to **3–25** bear in constructing your positive case. Concentrate in particular on the major and minor premises of their arguments: the legal principles on which they rely and the application of those principles to the facts of the moot problem. The following are the sorts of points that you should be looking for:

## Your opponents' authorities do not represent the law

You may be able to argue that the authorities cited by your opponents do not reflect the current state of the law. For example, a reported case may be inconsistent with another decision made by a court higher up the judicial hierarchy. You may even be lucky enough to find that one of your opponents' authorities has been expressly doubted, criticised or not followed in a subsequent case. Alternatively, you might notice that your opponents are relying on a case that was decided without reference to an inconsistent *earlier* authority that the court ought to have taken into account. Decisions of this sort are said to have been made *per incuriam* (literally, "through lack of care"). They arise most often in relatively lowly courts where counsel and the judiciary are more prone to overlooking existing case law.

## Your opponents have misread their authorities

You may accept that a reported case cited by your opponents was correctly decided, but still argue that they have drawn the wrong principle from it. You might notice, for example, that your opponents are pinning their faith on a passage in a judgment that does not accurately reflect the decision that the court made; other parts of the same judgment may be inconsistent with it or the judge may have been in the minority of a multi-member tribunal. Similarly, you may find that your opponents are relying on statements that are mere *obiter dicta* and form no part of the *ratio* of the decision. These passages are of limited weight and may readily be "trumped" by the authorities on which your team relies.

---

[8] At the same time, of course, you will be drafting the notes that you take with you to the moot and practising your oral submissions. You may also be preparing copies of your authorities for the judge if you were not required to serve them earlier. These topics are discussed in Chapters 5 to 7.

## Your opponents' authorities are distinguishable

Even if you accept that an authority cited by your opponents correctly sets out a relevant legal principle, you may be able to contend that it does not apply to the moot problem. Judges sometimes state that their findings should be limited to the particular facts of the cases before them. Statements of this type are manna from heaven if you are attempting to distinguish an unhelpful decision. Even if your opponents' authority is not expressly limited in this way, you may find that its facts differ in one or more material respects from the facts of the moot problem. A difference in fact is material in this sense if it would have altered the court's reasoning in some way.

## Your opponents' arguments are contrary to policy

Arguments based on supposed policy considerations are often the last resort of the desperate mooter. They are not without their uses, however, particularly if the policy alluded to has been expounded frequently by the courts. An example is the oft-expressed policy of the English courts that novel categories of negligence should only develop incrementally and by analogy with established categories.[9] In a moot concerned with the law of negligence, you might be able to contend that your opponents' arguments fall foul of this policy because they would result in a significant extension of the categories of negligence.

Another common policy argument, which is of more general application, goes something like this: if the court allows your opponents to succeed in this particular case, it will open the floodgates to a deluge of similar claims by other litigants. This can be a powerful point. But if you use it as part of your refutation, be ready to explain precisely why the "floodgates" would open if the court were to accept your opponents' argument.

## Taking effective notes

**3–26** Throughout the four phases of the research process described above, you should take comprehensive and comprehensible notes. Much of the effort expended in conducting your research will be wasted if your notes are so poor that you cannot rely on (or even understand) them when you come to prepare your oral submissions and any skeleton argument.

It is particularly important that you make effective notes about the leading cases that you uncover. Unless you are blessed with an elephantine memory, you will find that the details of even the most factually gripping case slip from your mind very soon after you read it. And as for those 100-page-plus auditors' negligence cases, you will do well just to remember what the previous paragraph was about.

**3–27**    To be of most use to you, your notes on key reported cases should include the following information:

---

[9] This policy is referred to, for example, by Lord Bridge of Harwich in *Caparo Industries plc v Dickman* [1990] 2 AC 605, 618.

- **The citation**
  Head your notes for each case with the full case name and law report citation (or citations if the case appears in more than one series of law reports). A complete and accurate citation will enable you to find the authority quickly in future.

- **The court in which the case was decided**
  This will help you to work out the relative importance of the cases that you find and, in particular, whether the moot court is bound by them.

- **A summary of the principal facts**
  You can usually keep this short. Make a note of the central facts and any unusual or amusing feature of the case that may help to jog your memory. You should descend to greater detail if you are likely to cite the case at the moot because the judge may ask for a summary of the pertinent facts during your oral submissions.[10]

- **A synopsis of the court's reasoning**
  Identify briefly the point or points of law that the court considered, the decision that it reached and its principal reasons for doing so.

- **The important references**
  Note the page or paragraph references of the most important passages of each judgment. You may have to find these again before the moot and you will not want to re-read the entire report.

# Five common mistakes

As the authors of this tome know only too well from long (and occasionally bitter) personal experience, there are plenty of mistakes to be made when conducting research for moots. The purpose of this section is to identify five of the most common errors that mooters make and to suggest how you can avoid them. **3–28**

## Under-estimating the time that research will take

Mooters sometimes fail to appreciate just how long it takes to research a moot problem properly. The issues that moot problems raise have often been pondered long and hard by many senior lawyers and judges. It is consequently no mean feat for a student to get to grips with them. Do not therefore be surprised if your researches take far longer to complete than you anticipate when you first read the moot problem. You should certainly shy away from setting arbitrary limits on the amount of time that you will spend on your research. Indeed, there is only one rule that determines how long your research will take: it will expand to fill the time available to conduct it. **3–29**

## Believing that there is a solution to the moot problem

Some mooters fall into the trap of thinking that, if they search carefully enough, they will find a reported case that comprehensively determines the law in their favour. This is to misunderstand the nature and purpose of mooting. Moot problems are designed to have no **3–30**

---

[10] Chapter 10 discusses how mooters should refer to authorities during their oral submissions.

clear answer. Indeed, the availability of arguable points for both sides is essential if the moot problem is to bring out the best in the participants.

This feature of moot problems means that you should not treat your research as a quest for a single decided case that will provide the "answer" to the moot problem. You will not find it. What you may find, of course, is a reported decision on which the moot problem appears to have been modelled. But there will always be some way of distinguishing that decision, whether on the basis that there are important differences in the central facts or that there are other reported cases that cast doubt on its correctness.

## Failing to see the wood for the trees

3–31  One of the most enjoyable aspects of researching the law for moots is tracking down authorities—the investigative element referred to earlier in this chapter. But mooters must make the most of the limited research time at their disposal. Little will be gained, for example, from detailed research into the historical origins of legal principles. There might well be a fascinating tidbit in the works of the Roman jurist Tribonian, but your moot judge is unlikely to thank you for reciting it. Nor will there be any material benefit in protracted research into the case law of distant jurisdictions with no track record of influencing the courts in this country. A decision of the first instance court of St Helena, however similar on the facts it may be to the moot problem, is not going to score you many points with the moot judge.

Whilst it is perfectly sensible to follow leads, even if initially unpromising, you should take stock from time to time. Ask yourself where your research is going, what it is uncovering, whether you will be able to use any of it at the moot and whether it is preventing you from researching more promising avenues. If your efforts are proving largely unproductive, you will probably make better use of your time by following a different line of inquiry.

## Failing to see the wood for the paper

3–32  As your research progresses, you should supplement your notes with hard copies of the leading authorities, whether from the photocopier or the computer printer. You will then have a permanent record of your research and be protected from the risk that your source material is not available the next time that you head to the law library.

Your copying should be kept under control, however. You should not be reproducing whole chapters of textbooks nor do you need to obtain copies of every case report that you read. If you take that course, you will quickly find yourself suffocated by a mass of paper, relatively little of which will provide any real assistance. And that is to say nothing of breaching the laws of copyright.

## Failing to work as a team

3–33  If you have a mooting partner, you should meet as often as you reasonably can to discuss the progress that you are making with your research. Regular get-togethers will provide an opportunity to work through any difficulties that you encounter. Very often, the best way of finding solutions to legal problems is to explain them to someone else. Sometimes, the "problem" then reveals itself not to be an issue at all. On other occasions, the act of describing the problem brings forth a means of dealing with it. You may even find that your partner comes up with an elegant solution. And if all else fails, and the problem remains intractable, at least you have a shoulder to cry on.

# A worked example

The research skills described in this chapter may be illuminated by a short example. Set out **3–34** below is therefore a description of how you might go about researching the first ground of appeal in the illustrative moot problem of *Cecil v Dickens* if you were acting on behalf of the appellant, Mr Dickens. Needless to say, the process described here is a much-abridged version of what you would actually do in practice.

The text of *Cecil v Dickens* appears in full in Chapter 2. The first ground of appeal states that, "*No duty of care arose in negligence*". As counsel for the appellant, your objective would be to build a case in support of that statement.

## Phase 1: understanding the legal context

As you would realise on your first read through the moot problem, the broad issue brought **3–35** into play by the first ground of appeal is the existence of a duty of care in negligence. The first phase of your research would accordingly focus on understanding what a duty of care is and the principles that determine when a duty of care arises.

Following the advice given earlier in this chapter, you might look for this understanding in the leading English law practitioner textbook on tort, which is *Clerk & Lindsell on Torts*.[11] Negligence is discussed in Chapter 8, with duty of care examined at para. 8–05 to 8–118. Many of these paragraphs are irrelevant for this purpose, however, and could accordingly be skipped. In fact, the only sections of real interest are the discussions of the nature of the duty of care concept (para. 8–05 to 8–11), the test for duty of care (para. 8–12 to 8–26) and duty of care where financial loss has resulted from reliance or dependence (para. 8–83 to 8–107). You would also have to consult the corresponding paragraphs of the supplement to the 19th edition.

This reading amounts to about 40 pages. It would provide an excellent grounding in the **3–36** overarching principles that govern the existence of duties of care in negligence including the various tests that the courts have applied. You would also see that para. 8–107 of *Clerk & Lindsell* contains a discussion about the specific issue raised by the first ground of appeal in *Cecil v Dickens*, namely whether a duty of care to avoid economic loss can arise where the relationship between the parties is social. That paragraph identifies two reported cases in which this issue was specifically considered: *Spring v Guardian Assurance plc* (*Spring*)[12] and *Chaudhry v Prabhakar* (*Chaudhry*).[13] These cases could form the beginnings of your running list of potentially relevant authorities.

---

[11] Table 3.5 lists the leading English law practitioner texts in eight subject areas including tort.
[12] [1995] 2 AC 296.
[13] [1989] 1 WLR 29.

## Phase 2: conducting detailed research

3–37   The second phase of the research process might begin with a search through the sources available to you for cases other than *Spring* and *Chaudhry* in which the English courts have considered whether a duty of care to avoid pure economic loss can arise in social situations. You would find very little, however, so you might next research in detail the general principles that govern the existence of duties of care when a person's negligence causes pure economic loss. There is an enormous amount of material on this topic. You would find, in particular, that in June 2006 the House of Lords reviewed the relevant principles in *Commissioners of Customs and Excise v Barclays Bank plc (Barclays)*.[14] You would therefore add this case to your running list.

As some point during your detailed research, you would read the *Spring*, *Chaudhry* and *Barclays* decisions. You would discover as follows:

- In *Spring*, the House of Lords held that an employer who gives a reference to a former employee owes a duty of care in its preparation. However, two members of the House of Lords (Lords Slynn and Woolf) doubted whether the giver of a reference to a social acquaintance would owe a duty of care. This case is therefore broadly helpful.

- In *Chaudhry*, the Court of Appeal held that a family friend *did* owe a duty of care to a woman whom he helped to find her first car. This case is therefore broadly unhelpful to your side of the argument, but highly relevant because your opponents might well cite it as one of their authorities.

- In *Barclays*, the House of Lords used all three of the following tests to determine whether a duty of care arose to avoid pure economic loss: (1) whether the defendant had "assumed responsibility" for the claimant; (2) whether the so-called "three-fold" test applied in *Caparo Industries plc v Dickman (Caparo)*[15] had been satisfied (i.e., the loss was foreseeable, there was a relationship of proximity between the parties and it was fair, just and reasonable to impose a duty); and (3) whether the imposition of a duty of care would be "incremental" to previous cases. This decision is important because it illustrates the approach that the courts take when deciding whether to impose a duty of care in financial loss cases.

3–38   You would find that these decisions refer to a number of reported cases that would be worth adding to your running list and, in due course, reading. They include *Caparo, Hedley Byrne & Co Ltd v Heller & Partners Ltd (Hedley Byrne)*[16] and *White v Jones*.[17] Your detailed research might range in other directions too. The judgments in *Barclays* refer, for example, to three separate articles in the *Law Quarterly Review*. You might find some interesting material in them. You might also spend some time looking for relevant case law from overseas. Australia and New Zealand are particularly fertile sources of jurisprudence about negligence.

---

[14] [2006] UKHL 28; [2006] 3 WLR 1.
[15] *op. cit.*
[16] [1964] AC 465.
[17] [1995] AC 207.

# Phase 3: finalising arguments and selecting authorities

Whilst reading the material that you unearthed during your detailed research, you would **3–39** start to formulate arguments. As you would expect from a well constructed moot problem, there are numerous arguments available to both sides. By way of illustration,[18] figure 3.3 summarises one possible line of argument for your positive case.

## Figure 3.3: Possible line of argument

**3–40**

- The leading case is *Barclays*.
- Mr Cecil does not satisfy any of the tests applied by the House of Lords in *Barclays* for the following reasons:
  - The fact that Mr Dickens told Mr Cecil that he should consult litigation solicitors if he decided to pursue a claim against the accountants shows that Mr Dickens did not "assume responsibility" for Mr Cecil.
  - It was not reasonably foreseeable that Mr Cecil would wait for more than three years after speaking to Mr Dickens before he contacted litigation solicitors.
  - It would not be fair, just and reasonable to impose a duty of care on Mr Dickens given the social context in which he advised Mr Cecil. The context includes the friendship between the parties and the fact that the advice was given in a pub.
  - The imposition of a duty of care would not be "incremental" because *Cecil v Dickens* is quite different from other cases in which the courts have imposed duties of care to avoid pure economic loss, e.g., where an employer gave a reference to an employee (*Spring*) or where a solicitor failed to draft a will (*White v Jones*).

Having settled on a line of argument, you would need to draw up your list of authorities. Were you to employ the argument summarised in figure 3.3, your most important authority would be *Barclays*. It carries considerable legal weight, being a decision of the House of Lords, and it is of relatively recent vintage. If you were only able to select one authority, this might well be it. With more space on your list to play with, you might consider citing *Spring*, *Hedley Byrne* and para. 8–107 of *Clerk v Lindsell*.

# Phase 4: refuting your opponents' case

The arguments that you might come up with to refute the respondent's case would depend **3–41** on the authorities that they cited. If their research had been as careful as yours, however, it is safe to assume that their list of authorities would include *Chaudhry*. In the last phase of the research process, you would therefore want to find ways of undermining that decision. Figure 3.4 lists some of the arguments open to you.

---

[18] This line of argument provides the basis for part of the sample skeleton argument included in Chapter 4.

## Figure 3.4: Possible basis for refutation

**3–42**

> - *Chaudhry* was not unanimous because Lord Justice May doubted whether a duty of care arose. *Clerk & Lindsell* states that Lord Justice May was right.
>
> - The two judges in *Chaudhry* who held that a duty of care existed were heavily influenced by the fact that there was a relationship of agent and principal between the parties. No such relationship exists in *Cecil v Dickens*.
>
> - The facts of *Chaudhry* were very different from *Cecil v Dickens*. For example, whereas in *Chaudhry*, the defendant told the claimant that she did not need to have the car inspected by a mechanic, Mr Dickens told Mr Cecil to consult litigation solicitors if he wanted to proceed with a claim against the accountants.

# Primary sources for research

**3–43**   This final section describes briefly the primary sources of the information that you are likely to utilise when conducting research for moots. The precise resources at your disposal will obviously depend on the extent of the collection held at or accessible from the law library where you work. If you are to make the most of those resources, you will need to hone your online and paper-based research skills.

## Case reports

**3–44**   Case reports contain the full text of judgments in significant decided cases as well as a headnote for each decision. In the more authoritative series of law reports, including the *Law Reports*, the *Weekly Law Reports* and *Session Cases*, the authorities referred to in the judgments of the court are listed at the beginning of each report. The *Law Reports* and the *Weekly Law Reports* even go so far as to list the cases that counsel cited in argument, but that are not referred to in the court's judgments.

In addition to being authorities themselves, decided cases are a vital source of information about other authorities. Many higher court judgments, in particular, contain scholarly examinations of the law that refer not only to previously decided cases, both at home and abroad, but also to academic commentary in textbooks and journal articles.

## Practitioner textbooks

**3–45**   Practitioner textbooks are primarily aimed at the legal profession and are usually written by prominent practising lawyers or academics. They refer, sometimes at considerable length, to the leading decided cases and are often laden with lengthy footnotes containing references to reported cases and seminal journal articles.

Tables 3.5 and 3.6 list by subject area some of the most well-known English and Scots law practitioner textbooks. These are not, it should be recorded, definitive lists. In many areas of the law, there are other excellent practitioner textbooks that you may find just as useful.

## Table 3.5: English law practitioner textbooks

| Subject area | Textbook | Current edition |
|---|---|---|
| Company law | *Gore-Browne on Companies* | Loose-leaf |
| Contract law | *Chitty on Contracts* | 29th (2004) |
| Criminal law | *Archbold* | New edition annually |
| Equity and trusts | *Snell's Equity* | 21st (2005) |
| Land law | *Emmet on Title* | Loose-leaf |
| Private international law | *Dicey, Morris and Collins, The Conflict of Laws* | 14th (2006) |
| Sale of goods law | *Benjamin's Sale of Goods* | 7th (2006) |
| Tort law | *Clerk & Lindsell on Torts* | 19th (2006) |

**3–46**

## Table 3.6: Scots law practitioner textbooks

| Subject area | Textbook | Current edition |
|---|---|---|
| Company law | *Gore-Browne on Companies* | Loose-leaf |
| Contract law | *McBryde, The Law of Contract in Scotland* | 2nd (2003) |
| Criminal law | *Gordon, The Criminal Law of Scotland* | 3rd (2005) |
| Delict | *Walker, Delict* | 2nd (1981) |
| General | *Walker, The Law of Civil Remedies in Scotland* | (1974) |
| International private law | *Anton & Beaumont, Private International Law* | 2nd (1990) |
| Land law | *Gordon, Scottish Land Law* | 2nd (1999) |
| Trusts and succession | *Meston, Scottish Trusts and Succession Service* | Loose-leaf |

**3–47**

# Student textbooks

The best textbooks aimed at undergraduates contain accurate, accessible and reasonably full **3–48** descriptions of the law, and refer to all of the important reported cases. Unlike practitioner textbooks, however, it is difficult to identify the pre-eminent student texts. Nonetheless, it is probably safe to rely on any textbook that your tutors recommend for a particular subject.

# *Halsbury's Laws/The Stair Memorial Encyclopaedia*

*Halsbury's Laws of England* and *The Law of Scotland: Stair Memorial Encyclopaedia* are **3–49** encyclopædias of English and Scots law respectively. At the last count, *Halsbury's Laws* ran to 56 volumes not including indices and supplements,[19] and *The Stair Memorial Encyclopaedia* filled 25 volumes.

---

[19] The references here are to the fourth edition, which has also been through numerous reissues.

Since the range of *Halsbury's Laws* and *The Stair Memorial Encyclopaedia* is far wider than any individual textbook, you must search them effectively for information. It is beyond the scope of this work to explain how to conduct such a search, but there are several guides on the subject if you require assistance.[20]

## Journal/periodical articles

**3–50**   There is a bewildering array of legal journals and periodicals available to law students. They range from overtly academic publications like the *Law Quarterly Review* and the *Modern Law Review* to specialist practitioner periodicals such as *Computers & Law* and *The Journal of International Banking Law and Regulation*.

     The focus of most journal articles is very narrow, often a single decided case or a highly technical legal issue. As a result, searching journals should not form a major element of your pre-moot preparation. If you have the time, however, a quick, targeted search for potentially relevant articles can bear fruit. In particular, well researched articles frequently provide useful ideas for arguments and point you in the direction of decided cases that other sources miss, especially decisions of foreign courts.

## Lecture notes and handouts

**3–51**   Do not underestimate your lecture notes and handouts as sources of relevant authorities. Any law tutors worth their salt will ensure that the materials that they produce refer to the latest legal developments.

## Legal dictionaries

**3–52**   Some moot problems are concerned with the meanings of particular words or phrases. If you are faced with a moot problem of this sort, you should look up one or more of the leading legal dictionaries, in addition to a conventional dictionary. The most well-known English legal dictionaries are probably *Stroud's Judicial Dictionary*[21] and *Words and Phrases Legally Defined*.[22] Both of these works include references to reported cases in which the meanings of the defined words and phrases were judicially considered.

## Online sources

**3–53**   Many of the sources described above are available online. Although some databases can be accessed for free, the most comprehensive, and therefore the most useful for research purposes, are available only to subscribers. Your access will consequently depend on whether the law library at which you conduct your research has subscribed to them.

---

[20] For guidance on searching *Halsbury's Laws*, for example, see *Knowles and Thomas, op. cit.*, pp112–116.
[21] 5th ed (1986), with a supplement published in 1999.
[22] 3rd ed (1988), with a supplement published in 2005.

Web-based sources of legal information were virtually non-existent 10 years ago and the materials available online are increasing year-on-year. At present, however, the three most commonly available UK commercial databases are probably Westlaw UK, LexisNexis Butterworths and Lawtel. The key features of each are described briefly below. For a more detailed exposition both of what these databases contain and how to use them effectively, you should consult a specialist text.[23]

- **Westlaw UK**
  Westlaw UK provides access to UK case law and legislation as well as journals published by Sweet & Maxwell. Its case coverage extends to 21 series of law reports including the *Law Reports* and the *Weekly Law Reports*. Westlaw UK also contains a comprehensive collection of EU case law, including judgments handed down by the European Court of Justice and the European Court of First Instance.

- **LexisNexis Butterworths**
  LexisNexis Butterworths provides access to a range of databases covering, amongst other things, UK and EU case reports, UK legislation and legal journals published by Butterworths. It also includes a number of practitioner textbooks and *Halsbury's Laws*.

- **Lawtel**
  Lawtel is used principally by practitioners. Its great virtue is that it is updated daily with the most recent, often as yet unreported, court decisions. It therefore provides the very latest intelligence about the law. However, unlike Westlaw UK and LexisNexis Butterworths, Lawtel does not contain links to any series of law reports.

In addition to the subscription services described above, there are countless free databases **3–54** that provide access to case law and legislation. Two prime examples are the website of the British and Irish Legal Information Institute (*www.bailii.org*), which draws together publicly-available transcripts of recent decisions of certain English and Scottish courts (amongst others), and the website of the Office of Public Sector Information (*www.opsi.gov.uk*), which contains the full texts of all primary and delegated legislation enacted by the UK Parliament from 1987.

# Summary

This chapter has examined the skills required in order to research the law for moots and **3–55** construct persuasive legal arguments. Those skills are the *sine qua non* of effective mooting. Without them, you will have no chance of preparing and delivering compelling written and oral submissions. It is hoped that this chapter has helped you to acquire these skills. It has, in particular:

- Identified the components of a persuasive legal argument.

---

[23] See, for example, *Knowles and Thomas, op. cit.*, at pp7–18.

- Described the various steps involved in conducting research for moots.

- Explained how to avoid some of the common pitfalls of research.

- Listed the major sources of research material.

# 4 Skeleton arguments

Skeleton arguments are now ubiquitous in the English civil courts and many English law **4–1** mooting competitions require the participants to produce them. Drafting an effective skeleton argument is therefore a key skill for the modern English mooter as it is for the modern English practitioner. Whilst practitioners in Scotland routinely intimate "notes of argument" and "notes of basis" for court hearings, the authors of this text are unaware of any Scots law mooting competition that currently requires them. For that reason, this chapter focuses solely on English law. Much of what follows should nonetheless be relevant to Scottish mooters if and when the practice of drafting skeleton arguments is extended to Scots law mooting competitions.

This chapter begins by explaining briefly what a skeleton argument is. It then describes in detail what skeleton arguments should contain and how to go about drafting them. With the assistance of examples using the illustrative case of *Cecil v Dickens*, it will take you from the blank page, through the drafting process, to the finished article.

## What is a skeleton argument?

A skeleton argument is a written outline of your case. It should introduce the judge to the **4–2** issues that arise for determination at the moot and summarise briefly, but persuasively, all of the main arguments that your team intends to advance. It should also refer to each of the authorities on which your team relies.

Skeleton arguments are increasingly common in English law moots, a reflection of their growing importance in professional practice, particularly in the civil courts. Gone are the days when a judge's introduction to a case came when counsel rose to their feet at the beginning of a trial. Now, skeleton arguments are mandatory for all but the shortest of procedural hearings.

There are two main reasons for the burgeoning use of skeleton arguments in practice. The first is that skeletons enable judges to prepare more effectively for hearings. Since advocates must serve their skeletons on the court (and on each other) in advance of hearings, judges know beforehand what their cases are about and can identify the issues on which to focus when the advocates are on their feet. The second reason is that skeleton arguments promote fairness between the parties. Both sides know in advance roughly what the other will say and no-one is ambushed at the hearing. The advocates' oral submissions can then concentrate on the real issues in dispute.

If you are required to produce a skeleton argument for a moot, you are likely to find that **4–3** the competition rules contain a number of relevant provisions. Typically, for example, the rules will impose a page or word limit and require the teams to exchange their skeletons ahead of the moot (typically 24 or 48 hours beforehand). The rules of some mooting competitions even prohibit the participants from going "off piste" at the moot by making points that are not specifically presaged in their skeleton arguments.

# Basic structure of skeleton arguments

**4–4** There is a well-recognised lay-out for skeleton arguments. It applies as much to a 30–page skeleton drafted by counsel for a major court hearing as it does to a one-page skeleton prepared for the first round of a mooting competition. That structure is set out in barest outline in figure 4.1.

### Figure 4.1: Basic lay-out of a skeleton argument

**4–5**

| HEADING (including the parties and the court) |
|---|
| INTRODUCTION |
| SUBMISSIONS ON EACH GROUND OF APPEAL |
| CONCLUDING PARAGRAPH |
| Names of counsel |
| Date |

This template consists of four principal elements: the heading; the introduction; the submissions; and the conclusion. Each of these elements deserves closer attention, which is accorded to them in turn below.

# Heading

**4–6** The heading of your skeleton argument should enable the reader, particularly the moot judge, to identify quickly what the document is and the fictitious party on whose behalf it has been served. Ideally, you should adopt the form of heading illustrated by figure 4.2. It is a simplified version of the standard heading used by professional lawyers in England and Wales. It does not take up much space, so you should be able to use it even if your skeleton argument is subject to a tight page limit.

### Figure 4.2: Heading

**4–7**

IN THE COURT OF APPEAL (CIVIL DIVISION)

BETWEEN:

CHARLES DICKENS

Appellant

-and-

HENRY CECIL

Respondent

SKELETON ARGUMENT
ON BEHALF OF THE APPELLANT

You will see that the heading in figure 4.2 is arranged in a distinctive way and comprises **4–8** the following principal elements:

- **Identity of the moot court**
  The name of the court in which the moot is taking place is set out in the top left-hand corner of the heading and is underlined. For an English civil law moot, the moot court is usually the Civil Division of the Court of Appeal or the House of Lords. For English criminal law moots, the moot court is normally the Criminal Division of the Court of Appeal or the House of Lords.

- **Identity of the parties**
  The full names of the parties are set out in capital letters in the middle of the page with the descriptions of each (i.e., "Appellant" and "Respondent") appearing underlined on the right-hand margin. When identifying natural persons in headings, you should include their entire names without any titles (e.g., "FRED FELIX FLINTSTONE"). Only if the moot problem does not provide an individual's first name should you use "MR", "MS", "MRS" etc. as appropriate (e.g., "MRS FLINTSTONE"). If a party is a corporate person, you should include in the heading the word "LIMITED" or "PLC" as the case may be (e.g., "BARNEY'S BOULDERS LIMITED").

- **Order of parties' names**
  The parties should appear in the heading in the order appellant followed by respondent regardless of which side your team is representing. This order reflects the fact that the first advocate to address the judge at the moot will represent the appellant. This rule applies even if, as in *Cecil v Dickens*, the claimant in the proceedings is the respondent to the appeal.

- **The word "-and-"**
  In the centre of the page, between the parties' names, you should insert the word "-and-". Do not use the letter "v" or the word "versus". The former should be reserved for citing authorities and the latter for advertising boxing matches.

- **Identity of party on whose behalf the skeleton argument is served**
  Between "tramlines" below the names of the parties, the heading should state which party the skeleton argument is "on behalf of". Do not make the mistake of simply entitling your masterpiece "skeleton argument". The judge may then be forced to wade through the document to work out for himself which side's arguments it contains.

The heading of a skeleton argument drafted on behalf of a respondent would follow exactly the same format as figure 4.2 save in one respect: the word "APPELLANT" inside the "tramlines" would be replaced by the word "RESPONDENT".

# Introduction

Every skeleton argument should begin with a brief description of the case. In professional **4–9** practice, it is not uncommon to see skeletons with introductions lasting 10 pages or more (much to the chagrin of many judges). Thankfully, there is no call for such excess in a moot skeleton argument. Indeed, even if the competition rules impose no page limit on the length of your skeleton, you should keep your introduction short and sweet.

A common mistake amongst even relatively experienced mooters is to draft an introduction that repeats, often verbatim, some or even all of the facts recited in the moot problem. This is a waste of valuable space. The judge does not need to be told in your skeleton argument what the facts are; he can read them perfectly well in the moot problem. What the introduction to a moot skeleton argument can, and should, do is briefly set the scene for the judge. It should introduce the parties, explain in general terms what the case is about and state what you are asking the court to do.

Broadly speaking, there are two ways in which to approach the drafting of your introduction. One is to make it very brief, literally three or four lines. The other is to produce something a little longer that incorporates some of the factual background. The choice between the two will probably be dictated by the amount of space that the competition rules allow you.

## "No frills" introduction

4–10    The short form introduction provides a one-paragraph description of the case and requests the court to deal with it in the appropriate way, that is to say allow the appeal (if the skeleton argument is served on behalf of the appellant) or refuse the appeal (if it is served on the respondent's behalf). Figures 4.3 and 4.4 are example short-form introductions on behalf of the appellant and the respondent in *Cecil v Dickens*.

### Figure 4.3: Appellant's skeleton

4–11

> [Heading]
>
> 1.  This is an appeal against the decision of Steerforth J[1] upholding the claim of the Respondent ("Mr Cecil") against the Appellant ("Mr Dickens") for damages for negligent misstatement. Mr Dickens asks the court to allow the appeal on the basis that the learned judge's decision was wrong.
>
> . . .

### Figure 4.4: Respondent's skeleton

4–12

> [Heading]
>
> 1.  This is an appeal against the decision of Steerforth J upholding the claim of the Respondent ("Mr Cecil") against the Appellant ("Mr Dickens") for damages for negligent misstatement. Mr Cecil asks the court to refuse the appeal on the basis that the learned judge's decision was correct for the reasons that he gave.
>
> . . .

---

[1] This is the correct way to write the name of a High Court judge in a skeleton argument. There is a comparison of the written and spoken versions of judges' titles in Chapter 9.

As you can see, despite being drafted on behalf of opposing parties, these examples are almost identical. Both also demonstrate the use of definitions. Although by no means obligatory in skeleton arguments, definitions can greatly assist the judge. Constant references to "the Appellant" or "the Respondent" can be confusing. Names are more likely to stick in the memory. In figures 4.3 and 4.4, the parties have therefore been given their actual names; the appellant is referred to as "Mr Dickens" and the respondent as "Mr Cecil".

## "With frills" introduction

The long form introduction includes the information contained in the "no-frills" version, but **4–13** weaves into it fragments of the factual background. In doing so, however, it should lose none of the punchy quality of the short form introduction. What you are aiming for is something that resembles the opening of a Lord Denning judgment.

In drafting a long form introduction, it is important to ensure that any reference to the facts is accurate. The judge will probably read the moot problem before your skeleton and will not be impressed by an overly partisan description of the background. Of course, what you can, and should, do is highlight in your introduction the facts that support your submissions.

The illustrative case of *Cecil v Dickens* can again be employed by way of example. Figure 4.5 is a possible long form introduction to the skeleton argument of the appellant, Mr Dickens.

### Figure 4.5: Appellant's skeleton

**4–14**

[Heading]

1. In this case, the Respondent ("Mr Cecil") alleges that the Appellant ("Mr Dickens") provided negligent advice to him in the course of a conversation in a pub during 2002. Mr Cecil contends that, as a result of this advice, he failed to pursue a cause of action against a firm of accountants before the relevant limitation period expired three years later.

2. At first instance, Steerforth J held that Mr Dickens owed a duty of care to Mr Cecil and breached that duty by failing to warn Mr Cecil of the existence of the limitation period. Mr Dickens appeals against both of these findings and asks the court to allow the appeal on the basis that the learned judge's decision was wrong.

. . .

Note that this example specifically mentions the given fact that the conversation between Mr Cecil and Mr Dickens took place in a pub. This sets the scene for Mr Dickens's argument that it would not be fair, just and reasonable to impose a duty of care for advice given in a social context.[2] The first paragraph also makes the point that three years remained to run of the relevant limitation period when Mr Dickens advised Mr Cecil. This lays the foundation for Mr Dickens's argument that it was not foreseeable that Mr Cecil would wait for such a long time before attempting to issue proceedings against the accountants.

---

[2] Both of the arguments referred to in this paragraph come from the possible line of argument outlined in figure 3.3 in Chapter 3.

The focus of the skeleton argument on behalf of Mr Cecil would, of course, be rather different. Figure 4.6 is an example long-form introduction to his skeleton.

## Figure 4.6: Respondent's skeleton

4–15

> [Heading]
>
> 1. In the course of a conversation during 2002, the Respondent ("Mr Cecil") asked the Appellant ("Mr Dickens"), a qualified solicitor, how to claim compensation from a firm of accountants. Although Mr Dickens told Mr Cecil that he had an arguable claim, he failed to mention that a limitation period applied to it. The claim became statute barred without Mr Cecil issuing proceedings. He accordingly sued Mr Dickens for giving negligent advice.
>
> 2. At first instance, Steerforth J upheld the claim, finding that Mr Dickens owed a duty of care to Mr Cecil and that he breached that duty by failing to warn of the existence of the limitation period. Mr Dickens appeals against both of these findings. Mr Cecil asks the court to refuse the appeal on the basis that the learned judge's decision was correct for the reasons that he gave.
>
> . . .

The facts included in this example are rather different from those that appear in figure 4.5. In particular, there is no mention of the unhelpful facts that the vital conversation took place in a pub and that Mr Cecil failed to issue proceedings for three years. On the other hand, the introduction does state that Mr Dickens was a qualified solicitor. This fact will support Mr Cecil's arguments that he relied on Mr Dickens's professional expertise and that the standard of care that applied to Mr Dickens in giving advice was that of a solicitor rather than a non-professional.

# Submissions

4–16    The submissions are the heart of every skeleton argument. They should summarise your team's arguments on each ground of appeal. The focus of the submissions should be your team's positive case, which will already be well developed by the time you come to draft your skeleton. The submissions should say little, if anything, by way of refutation of the other side's case since you will not know at that stage what the detail of your opponents' arguments will be.

The next few pages examine how to draft submissions in skeleton arguments. This examination covers three topics: the keys to drafting effective submissions; referring to authorities in submissions; and some linguistic do's and don't's.

## Keys to effective submissions

4–17    Effective submissions are persuasive submissions. Persuasive submissions are concise, logical and accurate. If any one of this Holy Trinity falls by the wayside, the effectiveness of the submission will be compromised. Each of these keys to effective submissions is therefore considered separately below.

## Conciseness

Skeleton arguments should be short; they are not called *skeleton* arguments for nothing. **4–18** Your submissions should therefore be limited to the bare "bones" of your arguments. You may, of course, have no option but to write brief submissions if your skeleton is subject to a stringent page or word limit. But there are at least two good reasons for keeping your submissions concise even if you are free from such a restriction.

First, you need to hold something back for the moot. If you spell out every aspect of your argument in detail in your skeleton, you will leave yourself with nothing new to say during your oral submissions. You then face the danger that your speech becomes little more than a canter through your skeleton argument.

The second reason for keeping your submissions succinct is that you will have to exchange your skeleton argument with the other side in advance of the moot. Whilst formidable opponents will anticipate much of your positive case even before seeing your skeleton, there is no need to spoon-feed them the nitty-gritty. Let them spend some of their precious preparation time thinking about how the detail might flow from your written submissions, and force them to listen carefully to what you say at the moot.

The need to write concisely does not just apply to the length of the submissions in your **4–19** skeleton argument. It applies equally to the language that you use. Persuasive language is usually short and pithy. Convoluted language, by contrast, suggests that the point being made is weak or that the draftsman has not thought it through properly. Or both.

## Logic

In order to be persuasive, your submissions must convey the logic inherent in your **4–20** arguments. As we saw in Chapter 3, the logic behind a legal argument for a moot generally derives from deductive reasoning. Deductive reasoning involves three elements: a major premise; a minor premise; and a conclusion. When you draft skeleton arguments, you can incorporate these elements into your submissions in the following way:

**A: Major premise**   Identify the precise proposition of law that you are advancing and refer to the authority from which you contend that the proposition derives.

**B: Minor premise**   Explain how the proposition of law on which you rely applies to the facts of the moot problem.

**C: Conclusion**   State the conclusion that you contend results from the application of the proposition of law to the facts of the moot problem. This is the finding that you request the judge to make.

Each argument that you make in your skeleton should include all three of these steps, even if they appear in a different order. With practice, you will find your own style of expressing and arranging them. It might follow the $A + B = C$ format above. But it could equally, for example, state the conclusion up-front so that the submission takes the form $C = A + B$. Indeed, many advocates prefer this approach because it is bold and punchy, and the judge will understand from the outset where the submission is going.

What you must not do when drafting submissions is make the mistake (which some mooters make) of simply paraphrasing the grounds of appeal. A "submission" of this sort is, in reality, nothing more than a statement of the conclusion of your argument. It consequently lacks logical substance and will make little impact on the judge.

**4–21**     Your submissions must not only convey the logic of your argument, they must also be arranged in a logical order. Whilst common sense should point you in the right direction, make sure that you adhere to the following guidelines:

- **Address the grounds of appeal in the order that they appear in the moot problem**
  There will usually be at least two grounds of appeal in the moot problem and they will be set out in a particular order. Unless you have a very good reason for departing from this order, stick to it when you arrange the submissions in your skeleton argument. The author of the moot problem, usually a lecturer in law or a practitioner, will have given some thought to the order in which the grounds of appeal are arranged. There will therefore be logic behind it. The problem in the illustrative case of *Cecil v Dickens*, for example, identifies two grounds of appeal: the first is concerned with the existence of a duty of care; the second with whether any duty was breached. This is plainly the logical order for your written submissions because the issue of breach of duty arises only if a duty of care exists in the first place.

- **For each ground of appeal, lead with your strongest point**
  In relation to any particular ground of appeal, you may have two or more submissions to make. One of those submissions will usually be stronger than the other(s). You should lead with that point. In this way, your submissions should have the greatest possible impact on the judge. If the leading point is strong, the judge will be more inclined to regard your subsequent (and weaker) arguments as bolstering it.

*Accuracy*

**4–22**     Lawyers are perfectionists. Their stock-in-trade is accuracy of expression, as you would expect in view of the unpleasant consequences that can follow if the documents that they draft contain mistakes or ambiguities.

Your submissions must therefore be accurate. Whenever you refer to an authority, for example, the citation must be correct. If, having received your skeleton argument in advance of the moot, the judge trots off to the library to read a law report that you have cited only to discover that no case of that name appears in the volume to which your skeleton refers, you will not only have wasted the judge's time, you will also lose credibility. Ensuring that your citations of authority are accurate is all about attention to detail. In particular, you should not rely on citations of law reports contained in textbooks and articles. They often make mistakes. You should instead always check the primary source—the report itself.

It is not just your citations of authority that must be accurate. Any reference that you make in your written submissions must be correct. Do not, for example, misstate a fact set out in the moot problem. Your submissions must also be *written* accurately. They must therefore be spelled correctly, properly punctuated and free from grammatical errors. Of course, these particular facets of accuracy are relevant to the whole of your skeleton argument, not just the submissions.

# Referring to authorities

**4–23**   As explained at the beginning of this chapter, your written submissions should refer to each of the authorities on which your team will rely at the moot. In order to assist the judge and your opponents, every reference to authority in your submissions should be as precise as possible, preferably identifying the page or paragraph numbers of the relevant passages.

The following guidance on drafting references to authority focuses on three issues: the format of citations; citing cases that appear in multiple series of law reports; and quoting from authorities.

## Format of citations

There is no universally applied format for the citation of authorities in skeleton arguments. **4–24** Some advocates underline the names of parties in case citations, for example, while others use italics. It is nonetheless a good idea to follow the format for citation employed by the *Law Reports*, which is the most authoritative series of English case reports. The essential features of this style are set out below:

- **Reported cases**
  The names of the parties and the letter "v" that divides them are in italics. The remainder of the citation is not italicised. When reference is made to a particular page of a judgment, the page number is added at the end of the citation together (if appropriate) with the name of the judge. The result is a citation that looks like this:

    *Donoghue v Stevenson* [1932] AC 562, 580 per Lord Atkin

- **Unreported cases**
  The names of the parties appear as in reported cases, but they are followed by the word "unreported" in parenthesis and the date on which judgment was handed down, which is written long-hand. The citation thus appears as follows:

    *Martine v South East Kent Health Authority* (unreported), 25 February 1993

- **Textbooks**
  This form of citation refers, in the following order, to the author's name (in italics), the title (also in italics), the edition, the year of publication (in parenthesis) and the volume number (if appropriate). A page reference can be added thereafter. The following examples are textbook citations (as it were):

    *Dicey, Morris and Collins, The Conflict of Laws*, 14th ed (2006), vol 1, p1
    *Clerk & Lindsell on Torts*, 19th ed (2006), pp462–463

- **Journal articles**
  The full name of the author comes before the title of the article, which is placed in quotation marks. The journal citation comes next. No italics are used. The following is an example:

    Jane Stapleton, "Duty of Care and Economic Loss: A Wider Agenda" (1991) 107 LQR 249

Whatever format you employ when citing authorities, it is important that you are consistent throughout your skeleton argument. Do not use one format for your first citation and a different format for the next.

## Citing cases reported in multiple series

Cases are regularly reported in more than one series of law reports. For example, the Court **4–25** of Appeal's decision in *Chaudhry v Prabhakar*, which is relevant to the illustrative moot problem of *Cecil v Dickens*, is reported both at [1989] 1 WLR 29 and [1988] 3 All ER 718.

When faced with this situation, which citation should you use in your skeleton argument? The answer is that you should cite the report in the series that appears highest in the hierarchy of law reports listed in table 4.7.

## Table 4.7: Hierarchy of English law reports

**4–26**

| |
|---|
| *Law Reports* |
| *Weekly Law Reports* |
| *All England Law Reports* |
| Any other full text law report (for example, the *Lloyd's Law Reports*) |
| Any case summary or case note (for example, a Lawtel case summary) |

This hierarchy is not universally observed, even amongst practising lawyers. You are therefore unlikely to be penalised for using one of the lesser series of reports when a more authoritative alternative exists. However, the *Law Reports* and the *Weekly Law Reports* do have three distinct advantages over the other series. First, every judgment is approved for publication by the judge who gave it. There is accordingly a decreased risk of a mistake appearing in the text. Second, both the *Law Reports* and the *Weekly Law Reports* include summaries of the arguments of counsel. As discussed in Chapter 3, these summaries can be a fertile source of inspiration when conducting research for moots. Finally, the *Law Reports* in particular often include the judgments of both the lower and appeal courts in the same report.[3] You may consequently be saved the trouble of checking whether a particular decision was appealed. These considerations should encourage you to cite from the *Law Reports* and the *Weekly Law Reports* whenever possible.

## *Quoting from authorities*

**4–27** During your legal research, you may find an especially helpful passage in a particular authority that neatly encapsulates a point that you wish to make at the moot. It could be a statement of legal principle in a case report, for example, or a pithy summary of the law in a practitioner textbook. Space permitting, there is nothing to stop you from quoting the passage in your skeleton argument. If you take this course, however, the watchword is brevity. The imported text should be short—no more than about five lines. Remember that, if necessary, you can always take the judge through a much larger extract of the authority during your oral submissions at the moot.

If the moot problem turns on the construction of a particular statutory provision, it is usually a good idea to quote it in full in your skeleton argument. That advice holds good even if the provision is set out in the moot problem because the judge will still benefit from having the relevant wording in the same document as your submissions. Use common sense, however. If the statutory provision runs to more than five lines, it is likely to be too long to replicate in full. You should then consider quoting only the most important phrases.

---

[3] It was the absence of this feature that led the Court of Appeal to criticise the citation of the *All England Law Reports* in *Governor and Company of the Bank of Scotland v Henry Butcher & Co.* [2003] 2 All ER (Comm) 557.

# Some linguistic do's and don't's

There are certain ways in which submissions should be expressed and certain ways in which **4–28** they should not. Some of the most important of these linguistic rules are described below.

## Make submissions; do not offer opinions

Always remember that you are advancing an argument on behalf of a fictitious "client". Your role as an advocate is akin to that of a hired gun. You are one of the Magnificent Seven defending the little Mexican village, not one of the little Mexican villagers. Do not therefore express your submissions as if they were your own views. You should avoid phrases such as *"In my/our opinion, . . .", "It seems to me/us that. . .",* and *"I/We think that . . .".* In their stead, use the more impersonal *"In my/our submission, . . .", "It is submitted that . . .",* and *"The appellant/the respondent submits that . . .".*

## Avoid colloquialisms

Do not be tempted to indulge in jargon, slang and informal language generally. Expressions such as *"The bottom line is . . ."* and many others like it have no place in formal legal drafting and may very well irritate the judge. Although it is not always immediately obvious if a particular word or phrase offends against this principle, the general rule is *"if in doubt, take it out".* On the same theme, you should avoid contractions of words such as "can't", "don't", "won't" and "shouldn't".

## Steer clear of inflammatory language

Few judges, whether sitting in a moot court or any other court, are impressed by the use of extravagant adjectives such as "outrageous" and "appalling" to describe an opponent's case.[4] You should also be wary of describing the other side's position as "hopeless" since moot problems are deliberately designed to ensure that both teams have reasonable arguments to make. Remember that, even if your opponent's submissions really are "hopeless" and "appalling", you can be pretty confident that the judge will work this out for himself.

## Identify submissions in the alternative

You may have two distinct arguments on a particular issue, either of which could lead the judge to find in your favour. If you include them both in your skeleton argument, you should clearly signpost them as alternatives so that the judge is not confused by what may be two, apparently contradictory, submissions. Your signpost can take a number of forms. The most concise are to begin the second submission with the word *"Alternatively, . . ."* or the phrase *"In the alternative, . . .".*

---

[4] In *Sony Computer Entertainment Europe Limited v Commissioners for Her Majesty's Revenue and Customs* [2006] EWCA Civ 772; [2006] All ER (D) 164, for example, the Court of Appeal castigated a skeleton argument for its *"frequent and unnecessary resort to hyperbole".*

## Conclusion

**4–29**  Last and, in this instance, least comes the conclusion of the skeleton argument. The conclusion consists of a final paragraph (if space permits), followed by the names of the mooters who have prepared the skeleton argument and the date on which it was served.

## Final paragraph

**4–30**  It is entirely proper to end your skeleton argument with the last of your substantive submissions and to skip a final paragraph altogether. Nonetheless, if you have some, albeit limited, space at the end of your skeleton, it is worth rounding it off with a short sentence stating what it is that you want the court to do. There is no harm, after all, in applying the old adage, *"Tell 'em what you're going to tell 'em* (introduction); *then tell 'em* (submissions); *then tell 'em what you told 'em* (conclusion)". If you are representing the appellant, your final paragraph will request that the appeal be allowed. If you are acting for the respondent, it will ask the court to dismiss or refuse the appeal. The following sentence, amended as appropriate, will cover either eventuality: *"It is accordingly submitted that the appeal should be allowed/dismissed."*

If you have plenty of space to spare, you can draft a slightly more elaborate final paragraph that reiterates the particular finding or findings that you would like the moot court to make. Figure 4.8 shows a possible concluding paragraph in the skeleton argument of the appellant in *Cecil v Dickens*.

### Figure 4.8: Final paragraph

**4–31**

---

. . .

6.   For the reasons set out above, it is submitted that the court should allow the appeal and find that Mr Dickens owed no duty of care to Mr Cecil or, if he did, that he did not breach it.

. . .

---

## Names and dates

**4–32**  After the text, at the right-hand side of the final page of your skeleton argument, you should set out on separate lines the names of the members of your team in the order in which they will address the moot court. Below the names of the mooters, but on the left-hand side of the page, you should insert the date on which you serve your skeleton argument.

Figure 4.9 shows how the names and dates would appear on a skeleton argument served by a mooting team comprising CJ Stryver as leading counsel and Sydney Carton as junior counsel.

**Figure 4.9: Names and dates**

4–33

6. [Final paragraph]

CJ Stryver
Sydney Carton

19 January 2007

## Presentation of skeleton arguments

Tempting though it may be to believe that the judge will be interested only in the **4–34** forcefulness of the submissions contained in your skeleton argument, the truth is that he will also be greatly influenced by the way in which those submissions are packaged. Presentation, in other words, matters hugely. This may sound like a depressing homily to style over substance, but it is no more than a recognition of the plain fact that presentation is just as important in written advocacy as it is in oral advocacy.

The good news is that it really is not that difficult to get the format of a skeleton argument right. Indeed, the surprising thing is that so many advocates, even those in professional practice, seem to get it so wrong.[5] What follows is a brief checklist of the "rules" of presentation:

- **Type it up**
  If at all possible, serve your skeleton argument in typewritten rather than manuscript form. In these days of omnipresent PCs, this may be an unnecessary exhortation, but, however neat your handwriting may be, a typed document will always be easier on the eye and look more professional.

- **Write on one side of the page only**
  Keep the text of your skeleton argument to one side of the sheet and leave the other side blank. You might be a radical environmentalist hell-bent on minimising paper waste, but the judge may not share your sentiment.

- **Use paragraph numbers**
  Make sure that every paragraph of your skeleton argument is numbered consecutively. This will allow the judge to find particular passages quickly and without fuss when you refer to them at the moot.

- **Insert page numbers**
  For the same reason, any skeleton argument that exceeds one page should be consecutively numbered at the bottom of each page.

---

[5] For a judge's take on the repeated failures of the barristers appearing before him to produce skeleton arguments in an appropriate format, see Mr Justice James Hunt, "The Anatomy Lesson", Counsel, February 2002.

- **Allow generous spacing and margins**

  If possible, your skeleton argument should be double-spaced and have decent margins on either side of the page. There are two main reasons for this. First, the judge (whose eyesight may not be what it once was) will find your skeleton easier to read. Second, you will give the judge some space on which to jot down notes.

- **Use headings**

  Even relatively short skeleton arguments benefit from two or three headings. For more lengthy skeletons, headings are essential if the judge is to make quick sense of the arguments that you are advancing. There is no need to go overboard, however. Headings are useful for distinguishing between the principal parts of your skeleton argument, such as the submissions on each ground of appeal and the conclusion. But their utility can be lost if every paragraph has one.

- **Avoid footnotes**

  Multiple footnotes may impress the authors of law reviews, but they are unlikely to endear you to a moot tribunal. The judge wants to understand from your skeleton argument what your case is without having to refer constantly to screeds of microscopic writing at the bottom of each page. Although the odd footnote can sometimes assist a skeleton argument, they are generally best avoided.

- **Avoid small or idiosyncratic fonts**

  If possible, you should stick to 11– or 12–pitch size and Times New Roman or Arial font when drafting your skeleton arguments. The judge should not have to pull out a magnifying glass to read your submissions. He may also question your sanity if your efforts are printed in a font that looks as though it was hand-written by a scribe. *This sort of thing, for example.*

- **Stick to the limit**

  As we have seen, most mooting competitions impose a page or word limit on skeleton arguments. You should respect it. Although you might be lucky and come up against a lenient judge who does not penalise minor overruns, do not count on it.

# Mistakes and how to deal with them

**4–35** It is possible to make all sorts of mistakes when drafting skeleton arguments. This short section examines two: errors of drafting, and missing the deadline for exchange.

## Mistakes in drafting your skeleton argument

**4–36** However many times you read your skeleton argument before exchange, you can never eliminate the possibility that it will harbour a mistake of some description. How you deal with that mistake if you discover it before the moot will depend on its seriousness and, potentially, the competition rules.

Below, in ascending order of magnitude, are three types of mistake that it is possible to make in a skeleton argument together with the approaches that you might sensibly consider taking to deal with them. None of these suggestions should be taken as gospel. As with most aspects of advocacy, you must apply common sense to the circumstances that confront you.

## Spelling and grammatical errors

Unfortunate though they are, your best policy is almost always to live with mistakes of this nature. However, if in the course of your oral submissions, you need to refer the judge to a passage of your skeleton argument that includes a spelling or grammatical error that in some way obscures the point that you were trying to make, you can always correct it "on the hoof".

## Incorrect citations

Mistakes of this type cannot be so easily ignored. If your skeleton refers to the wrong page or volume number of a law report, for example, the incorrect citation could cause considerable confusion to the judge and your opponents. In those circumstances, you should attempt to rectify the error as quickly as possible by notifying the judge and the other side of the correct citation. If they are not readily contactable, you may have to ask the moot organiser to let them know.

## Unarguable submissions

The worst case scenario is that you realise that one of the submissions in your skeleton argument is unarguable. Your opponents' skeleton might, for example, refer to a binding authority of which you were previously unaware that conclusively rebuts a submission that you have made. Be wary of reaching this conclusion too quickly, however. There is often a "heart in the mouth" moment when you see your opponents' skeleton for the first time. Inevitably, they will not have approached things in the same way as you; you may initially feel that their approach is more convincing. But that is very different from discovering that one of your submissions is wholly without foundation.

If that unfortunate eventuality does arise (and it should be a very rare event indeed), your best course is to deal with the point in oral submissions at the moot. If you can concoct an alternative way of arguing the point that does not suffer from the same fatal flaw, so much the better. If not, you can simply inform the judge that you are no longer pursuing the submission. You may even be able to turn the misfortune to your advantage if you can demonstrate to the judge your ability to accept the force of the other side's point, but then move the argument swiftly onto more solid ground.

# Missing the deadline for exchange

It will be apparent that errors of drafting are usually remediable in one way or another. It **4–37** may be more difficult to redress the damage done if you fail to exchange your skeleton argument on time. In professional practice, advocates who serve their skeleton arguments late are required to explain in a personal letter to the judge why they missed the relevant deadline. The consequences of late exchange in a moot can be similarly unwelcome. At the very least, the judge is likely to take late service of your skeleton into account in determining who wins the moot. In a close contest, compliance with the competition rules can be the deciding factor. Worse still is the possibility that, if the delay is significant, you may be forced to concede the moot altogether. The moot organiser is unlikely to take that step unless the competition rules are especially strict. But whatever the probability of this outcome, you do not want to take the chance that it will happen.

# The finished article

**4–38**  You now have the building blocks with which to construct a skeleton argument. So that you can see what the final edifice looks like, figure 4.10 is an example of a complete skeleton on behalf of the appellant in *Cecil v Dickens*. It draws together figures 4.2 (heading), 4.3 (appellant's short form introduction), 4.8 (final paragraph) and 4.9 (names and dates), and includes possible submissions on both grounds of appeal. The submissions on the first ground of appeal are based on the line of argument summarised in figure 3.3 in Chapter 3. Figure 4.10 assumes that the competition rules allow each team to cite just three authorities.

## Figure 4.10: Complete skeleton argument

**4–39**

IN THE COURT OF APPEAL (CIVIL DIVISION)

BETWEEN:

CHARLES DICKENS

Appellant

-and-

HENRY CECIL

Respondent

SKELETON ARGUMENT
ON BEHALF OF THE APPELLANT

1.  This is an appeal against the decision of Steerforth J upholding the claim of the Respondent ("Mr Cecil") against the Appellant ("Mr Dickens") for damages for negligent misstatement. Mr Dickens asks the court to allow the appeal on the basis that the learned judge's decision was wrong.

First Ground of Appeal: Duty of Care

2.  The modern approach to imposing duties of care to avoid pure economic loss is set out in *Commissioners of Customs and Excise v Barclays Bank plc* [2006] 3 WLR 1. The various tests applied by the House of Lords in that case are not satisfied here. In particular:

    (1) There was no assumption of responsibility because Mr Dickens expressly told Mr Cecil to consult other solicitors who specialised in litigation.

    (2) It was not reasonably foreseeable that Mr Cecil would delay for more than three years before consulting litigation solicitors.

    (3) It would not be fair, just and reasonable to impose a duty of care given that Mr Dickens provided advice to a friend in a social setting.

(4) The imposition of a duty of care would considerably extend liability in negligence for pure economic loss.

3. It is accordingly submitted that Mr Dickens owed no duty of care to Mr Cecil.

Second Ground of Appeal: Breach of Duty

4. If, contrary to his primary case, Mr Dickens owed a duty of care to Mr Cecil, the relevant standard of care is that of a reasonably competent solicitor specialising in conveyancing: *Green v Collyer-Bristow* [1999] Lloyd's Rep. PN 798. Further, Mr Dickens's duty was to take such care as was reasonable in the circumstances, not to take every possible care: *Winfield & Jolowicz on Tort*, 16th ed (2002) para. 11.24.

5. Mr Dickens satisfied the relevant standard when he told Mr Cecil to consult specialist litigation solicitors if he decided to pursue a claim against Wickfield's. It is accordingly submitted that Mr Dickens did not breach any duty that he owed.

Conclusion

6. For the reasons set out above, it is submitted that the court should allow the appeal and find that Mr Dickens owed no duty of care to Mr Cecil or, if he did, that he did not breach it.

CJ Stryver
Sydney Carton

19 January 2007

# Summary

The rules of many English mooting competitions now require the participants to produce **4–40** skeleton arguments. If drafted effectively, a skeleton will start the process of persuading the judge of the merits of your case and provide you with a solid foundation from which to launch your oral submissions. This chapter has explained the basic skills associated with preparing skeleton arguments. It has, in particular:

- Described what a skeleton argument is.

- Explained how to draft a persuasive skeleton.

- Advised on presentation.

- Recommended ways to address skeleton-related mistakes.

# 5 Notes for oral submissions

**5–1** Most mooters enter the moot courtroom clutching a sheaf of notes to assist them with their oral submissions. Yet, all too often, those notes prove to be more of a hindrance than a help. Many perfectly able advocates shackle themselves unnecessarily to full written speeches that they then proceed to read. Others take the opposite path, relying on minimal notes that leave them floundering for words at critical moments in their submissions.

This chapter explores the skills required to draft effective notes. It begins by exposing a few of the myths that surround notes and identifies the principal functions that notes should perform. It then analyses various styles of notes—full written speeches, outlines and ad hoc forms of notes—before offering a number of tips for note-drafting that apply whichever style you adopt. The chapter concludes by examining the various media on which notes can be written.

## Some myths about notes

**5–2** Few aspects of mooting have generated as much hokum as the notes that mooters prepare for their oral submissions. Even a relatively cursory surf on the internet uncovered the following dubious pronouncements on the subject:

- *"It is advisable . . . always to use cards rather than paper."*

- *"Barristers in practice . . . rarely speak from more than the skeleton argument that they have exchanged with the other side."*

- *"In no circumstances should you have a 'speech' written out in full."*

None of this is accurate. Whilst using cards works for some mooters, most prefer other media for their notes. Although there may be the odd practising advocate who occasionally speaks from nothing more than a skeleton argument, the vast majority do not. And whilst relying on a full written speech undoubtedly carries its share of risks, it is certainly not a bar to effective advocacy.

In truth, drafting notes for oral submissions is a matter of personal preference; more so, perhaps, than any other skill described in this book. The critical consideration is whether the notes that you prepare work for you. Do they, in other words, fulfil all of the functions that effective notes must perform?

# Functions of notes

Whether your notes are brief or bloated, typed up or scribbled in manuscript, they should **5–3** play three principal roles: a prompt; a flexible reference; and a comfort blanket. Although there is a significant overlap between them, each of these roles is discussed separately below.

## A prompt

Speaking in public has a strangely deleterious effect on the brain. Submissions that you may **5–4** have virtually (or even actually) memorised in the build-up to the moot can evaporate from your mind at the very moment when you need to recall them. And even if you do not suffer a complete mental block, you may find that *le mot juste* fails to materialise *juste* when you are attempting to deliver your most potent lines.

The first task of your notes is therefore to provide you with a prompt. As you are speaking, you should be able to look down at your notes, find the right place and be reminded of the information that you need in order to make your next point to the judge. If your notes are an effective prompt, you will be able to do all of this quickly and with minimal interruption to your train of speech. Conversely, signs that your notes are not providing a sufficient prompt include running out of things to say, punctuating your oral submissions with frequent "ums" and "errs", losing the thread of your argument and failing to maintain eye contact with the judge.

## A flexible reference

One of the most challenging aspects of mooting is having to adapt your oral submissions as **5–5** events unfold at the moot. You are most likely to be blown off course by interventions from the judge. His questions may force you to recast a submission that you were going to make or to re-order some of your points. You might also have to spend more or less time on a particular topic than you had originally intended, perhaps because your opponents have unexpectedly "majored" on it in their oral submissions or because they have ignored it altogether.

The second function of your notes is therefore to provide a flexible reference. Notes with the requisite degree of flexibility will allow you to jump around from one topic to another without losing your place. They will also enable you to compress or expand your submissions as the clock requires.

## A comfort blanket

Mooting is a stressful business. It requires a high degree of concentration, involves the **5–6** marshalling of numerous facts and documents, and takes place in public. The third task of your notes is therefore to offer you a modicum of comfort, a safe haven to which you can retreat if your memory fails you or your composure is momentarily rattled. Plenty of mooters have little need of a metaphorical comfort blanket, being naturally self-assured. But many, probably most, do like to have something to fall back on if they get into difficulty during their oral submissions.

# Styles of notes

5–7    Although there are doubtless mooters out there who have perfected the art of making sensational oral submissions from nothing more than a flow chart, most ordinary mortals' notes fall into one of three categories: a full written speech; an outline; or something more ad hoc. Each of these styles of notes is therefore examined below. None should be regarded as the paradigm. Different styles of notes work equally effectively for different people. What counts is not so much the form that your notes take as the way in which you use them.

## Written speeches

5–8    A written speech is a longhand version of the words that the mooter intends to speak at the moot; it is, in effect, a script for the mooter's oral submissions. Figure 5.1 provides an example of what the opening minute or so of the notes of the first mooter for the appellant in *Cecil v. Dickens* might look like if they were written out in full.

### Figure 5.1: Example written speech

5–9

> My Lord, I appear on behalf of the appellant in this matter, Mr Charles Dickens, together with my learned friend Sydney Carton. The respondent, Mr Henry Cecil, is represented by my learned friends Sally Mannering and Roger Thursby.
>    This is the hearing of the appeal against the decision of Mr Justice Steerforth sitting in the Queen's Bench Division that the appellant gave negligent advice to the respondent in relation to a potential claim by the respondent against a firm of accountants called Wickfield's.
>    The appellant appeals against the decision of the learned judge on two grounds. The first is that he owed no duty of care to the respondent. I intend to address Your Lordship on this ground of appeal. The second is that, even if a duty of care was owed to the respondent, the appellant did not breach it. My learned friend Mr Carton will address Your Lordship on this ground of appeal.
>    . . .

This style of notes certainly provides the greatest level of comfort. If you are stricken with nerves or your memory freezes, you can revert to your speech and plough on to the bitter end. It may not be pretty and it may not win you the moot, but you will at least have made it through your oral submissions. It is no doubt for this, entirely understandable, reason that most novice mooters tend towards this approach when drafting their notes.

5–10    Whilst a written speech is the ultimate comfort blanket, it is considerably less effective as a prompt. With your submissions written out in full sentences, you may not be able to deviate from the prepared text. Unless you memorise large tracts of your script (as some mooters do), you may then find it hard to lift your eyes from the page. With your head almost constantly down, you will struggle to project your voice effectively and to maintain eye contact with the judge. If you read your written speech, your delivery also runs the risk of sounding unnatural and stilted. People often find it difficult to write in precisely the way that they speak. Even if you possess that skill, it is no easy matter to read a speech lasting 10 minutes or more without once tripping over a word or phrase. If the judge picks up that you are reading from a speech, he may mark you down, however compelling the substance of your submissions may be.

If written speeches make poor prompts, they are even less flexible. Being overly reliant on a written speech makes it hard to compress or expand your oral submissions to adapt to circumstances at the moot. You will also have trouble reformulating your arguments in order to meet head-on a question from the judge or a point made by your opponents. In addition, when faced with a judicial intervention, the speech enthusiast may struggle to locate the section of his notes that he needs in order to provide a cogent response. It may be an even greater challenge to re-find the place from which to resume his submissions. Many is the mooter in this situation who has mistakenly returned to the wrong spot in his script and ended up re-reading a paragraph or two without realising it.

Drafting a full speech therefore has its pitfalls. Many of them can be avoided, however, if you take suitable precautions. Memorising sections of your speech will help, for example. You can also develop a system for maintaining the right place in your notes when the judge intervenes and you need to jump to a different section. It might be as simple as keeping your finger pressed to the spot that you had reached in your script. Alternatively, you might mark that point with a pen or a highlighter.

If you can manage the drawbacks effectively, it is perfectly possible to make persuasive— **5-11** and winning—submissions using this style of notes. Indeed, there are plenty of successful QCs who write out in advance virtually every word that they utter in court. And do not take our word for it. One of the luminaries of the English libel bar, which is hardly a bastion for the faint-hearted, described his method of preparing for hearings in this way: *"I type up every single word of my speeches including the apparent ad libs and asides. . . . I avoid lawyers' words at all costs and will rewrite a speech ten times until it fits."*[1]

## Outlines

At the other end of the note-drafting spectrum from the full written speech is the outline. **5-12** An outline is a way of organising your ideas on paper that conveys the logic and structure of your argument, often without resorting to complete sentences. It generally consists of a series of assertions and references placed on the page in several levels of indentation. Its success as a form of notes largely depends on the mooter's ability to strike the right balance between excessive detail and insufficient information. You can see an example of an outline in figure 5.2. It covers the same opening remarks that appeared as a full written speech in figure 5.1.

---

[1] *The Times*, 29 November 2005. The barrister quoted is John Kelsey-Fry QC.

## Figure 5.2: Example outline

**5–13**

> I.  Introductions
>
>     A.  Representing appellant, Charles Dickens
>
>         1. me
>
>         2. Sydney Carton
>
>     B.  Representing respondent, Henry Cecil
>
>         1. Sally Mannering
>
>         2. Roger Thursby
>
> II. Overview of appeal
>
>     A.  First instance
>
>         1. Judge: Steerforth J, QBD
>
>         2. Decision: appellant gave negligent advice to respondent re. potential claim by respondent against firm of accountants, Wickfield's
>
>     B.  Grounds of appeal
>
>         1. Appellant owed no duty of care (me)
>
>         2. Even if duty of care owed, appellant did not breach it (Mr Carton).
>
> . . .

An outline is a very flexible form of notes. The simplistic layout, with multiple headings and indentations, but much less text than a written speech, makes outlines easy to scan quickly. As a result, you can readily jump around your notes. If, for example, the judge asks a question about a point that you intend to deal with later in your submissions, you should be able to skip quickly to the relevant section of your notes. Once you have answered the judge's point, you can then launch straight back into your planned submissions without having to find a particular sentence. Greater flexibility also makes time management more straightforward because submissions can easily be curtailed or even dropped as the circumstances demand.

**5–14**    As long as it is sufficiently detailed, an outline can be an excellent prompt. The absence of dense text presents the information that you require in an accessible format that should enable you to lift your eyes from the page with routine frequency. You can then concentrate on engaging the judge eyeball to eyeball. Your prompt will also allow you freer rein than a written speech in your choice of words. Your delivery should accordingly appear to be "off the cuff" and the "clunkiness" often associated with relying on a script should be avoided. What is more, with vocabulary to find and arguments to articulate, there is little chance that you will slip into "autopilot" as some speech-readers do. You will simply have to concentrate too hard for your mind to wander.

The great drawback of an outline is that it has a low comfort factor. Instead of having a script to work from, you must come up with the words that you speak as you go along. The less detailed your outline, the more thinking that you will have to do on your feet. What you gain in spontaneity when all goes well can quickly be lost if one of two disasters strikes. The first is running out of things to say. This phenomenon is not, it should be stressed, confined to mooters who rely on outlines. It is more often a sign of nerves or lack of preparation than of insufficient notes. But there is unquestionably a correlation between the volume of notes and the risk of a protracted pause in a mooter's oral submissions: the fewer the notes, the greater the risk.

The second danger of relying on a sparse outline is the opposite of the first. Without **5–15** sufficient guidance from your notes, you may start to ramble. Amid the waffle, the judge, and possibly you yourself, may lose the thread of the argument and its persuasive force will be diminished. A particularly unfortunate feature of this failing is that, unlike drying up, which is usually blindingly obvious to all concerned, you may not realise that you are wandering from the point. Wrongly assuming that your submissions are hitting the mark, you may then continue for some time, blissfully unaware that your chances of winning the moot are receding with every convoluted sentence that you utter.

# Ad hoc notes

You do not have to choose between drafting a full speech and relying on nothing more than **5–16** an outline. You can instead draft notes in a style that is tailored to suit your particular needs.

Say, for example, that you like the comfort that a full written speech affords, but want to encourage yourself to look up more often from your notes. You might then write out your speech in full, but capitalise, underline or bolden certain key words or phrases in each sentence. The highlighted sections of your notes should then serve as prompts when you glance at the page, but you could still revert to your script if necessary. Similarly, you might insert headings or make liberal use of indentations in your written speech. With the text broken up, you should find it easier to scan quickly.

On the other hand, you might be keen to work from an outline for most of your oral submissions, but wish to leave nothing to chance at certain key points in your speech. You might, for example, be particularly concerned about your opening remarks, since it is relatively easy to become tongue-tied before you hit your stride. One solution is to supplement your outline by writing out in full the first few sentences of your submissions. You could take a similar approach elsewhere in your notes. You might, for instance, write out word-for-word any particularly complicated fact or legal principle that you intend to mention to the judge.

Figure 5.3 provides an example of another possible style of ad hoc notes. Like an outline, it makes liberal use of indentations. Where possible, it also uses abbreviated forms of words and initials, two note-reduction techniques that are discussed later in this chapter. Once again, this example covers the opening remarks that appear in long hand in figure 5.1.

## Figure 5.3: Example ad hoc notes

**5–17**

My Lord,

I appear A = Charles Dickens w/ Sydney Carton

R = Henry Cecil

    – represented: Sally Mannering & Roger Thursby

Intro.

This is appeal v. decision of Steerforth J. (QBD) that:

    – A gave neg. advice to R

    – re. pot. claim v. acc, Wickfield's

> A appeals on 2 grounds:
> - no DOC to R: I address
> - even if DOC, no breach: Mr Carton will address

Of course, these are only a selection of examples of how you might customise your notes. There are many other ad hoc styles, including bullet points and combinations of text and diagrams. You could use any of them. Just so long as they work for you on the day of the moot.

# Tips for improving your notes

5–18    Whichever style of notes you adopt, you should constantly be on the look out for ways to make them more user-friendly. This process is largely a matter of trial and error. If you can learn from watching other people's errors (or other people's trials for that matter), so much the better. What you must be prepared to do, however, is experiment.

The next few pages offer a handful of suggestions for improving the effectiveness of your notes. They should work whether your notes take the form of a full written speech, an outline or something altogether different.

## Develop note-reduction techniques

5–19    As a general rule, you should aim to reduce the length of your notes. The shorter they are, the more manageable they ought to be; you will be juggling fewer pieces of paper and will consequently be able to find your way around them more easily.

There are various devices that you can employ to reduce the length of your notes. A selection is summarised below.

### Drop extraneous linking words and expressions

5–20    This suggestion covers conjunctions such as "and" and "but", the words "that" and "which", the definite and indefinite articles ("the" and "a"), and certain common verbs. As anyone conversant with text messaging will know, very few of these words are necessary to make sense of a sentence. By taking them out, you not only save space, you also increase the spontaneity of your submissions because you are unlikely to use precisely the same language at the moot as you have used whilst practising beforehand.

### Replace words with symbols

5–21    An obvious example is the word "therefore", which is readily comprehensible as " = >" or as three dots in the form of a triangle. Similarly, the word "paragraph" can be written as "§". There are numerous other possibilities. Some do not greatly reduce the amount of text, but they invariably improve its readability.

## *Use initials*

You can drastically shorten the names of particular institutions and certain phrases by **5–22** initialising the constituent words. You can also initialise individual words. Table 5.4 contains a short list of examples, some of which were employed in the ad hoc notes in figure 5.3. You should be able to come up with many more.

## Table 5.4: List of initials

**5–23**

| Initial(s) | Full version of word(s) |
|---|---|
| A | appellant |
| C | claimant |
| CA | Court of Appeal |
| ChD | Chancery Division |
| D | defendant or defender |
| DOC | duty of care |
| ECHR | European Court/Convention of/on Human Rights |
| ECJ | European Court of Justice |
| HC | High Court |
| HL | House of Lords |
| IH | Inner House of the Court of Session |
| JR | judicial review |
| OH | Outer House of the Court of Session |
| P | pursuer |
| QBD | Queen's Bench Division |
| R | respondent |
| 3P | third party |

## *Build a lexicon of abbreviations*

Most students develop their own form of shorthand at university as they jot down at high **5–24** speed the learned musings of their tutors. It is worth taking the time to develop this skill, and not just because it can be put to good use in drafting notes for oral submissions at moots. Some of the abbreviations that you adopt may be legal words or phrases, but most will have no specific connection to the law. Any good dictionary will contain a list of abbreviations that you can plunder as a starting point for your lexicon. Table 5.5 provides a few examples. Some are blindingly obvious; others, hopefully, less so.

## Table 5.5: List of abbreviations

5–25

| Abbreviation | Full version of word(s) |
|:---:|:---|
| a/c | account or accounts |
| acc | accountant |
| bar | barrister |
| co | company |
| diff | difference or different |
| dir | director |
| est | establish |
| exec | executive |
| gp | group |
| inc | include |
| jud | judge |
| neg | negligence or negligent |
| o/ | other or over |
| opp | opportunity |
| pot | potential |
| ref | reference or refer |
| sol | solicitor |
| u/ | under |
| w/ | with |
| wh/ | which |
| w/o | without |

# Leave space for supplementary notes

5–26    However well thought out your notes may be, you will probably want to supplement them during the moot. There is a good chance, for example, that you will think of a number of points in rebuttal as you listen to your opponents' submissions. Alternatively, you might feel that your team-mate has made a poor fist of answering a particular question from the judge, and decide that you should provide a more detailed response during your speech. In either of these events (and plenty of others), you will want to jot down in your notes the points that you wish to make so that you are reminded of them at the appropriate junctures in your oral submissions.

There are several ways of facilitating last-minute additions to your notes.

- **Leave a wide margin on each page of your notes**
  Your margin could extend to as much as half of each page, although a third might be more workable. You can then make manuscript insertions in the blank part of the page at precisely the point in your notes where you will need them.

- **Write your notes on one side of the page only**

  If your notes are contained in a counsel's notebook or a ring binder and you only write on one side of each page, you will have a blank page facing each page of notes. You can use it for additional notes. You might even use arrows to point from your supplementary notes to the precise spot in your original notes where the new material should be introduced.

- **Bring extra loose sheets of paper**

  Most mooters make their supplemental notes on additional sheets of paper rather than in the body of their main notes. This approach can work well, but it does lead to a proliferation of paper, which can be difficult to manage as you attempt to flit from original to supplementary notes and back again.

## Prepare notes for judicial interventions

Your notes should not be confined to the submissions that you would make if the judge **5–27** gives you a clear run during your speech. You should also draft notes to assist in dealing with the topics that you believe the judge is most likely to ask about. If one of those points comes up, you can then turn to your prepared notes. With a bit of luck, they will provide you with at least the basis for a coherent and convincing response.

As you will not be able to anticipate the *precise* questions that the judge will ask during your speech, the notes that you prepare for dealing with judicial interventions should be in outline or bullet point form. Not only will you be able to skim read them more quickly that way, you can also adapt your responses to fit the exact wording of the judge's questions.

Supplementary notes of this type are probably best placed at the end of your notes proper or on a separate sheet of paper. You will then have easy access to them if the need arises. You should identify them with readily recognisable subject headings.

## Prepare summaries of the cases you rely on

At some point during your oral submissions, and often more than once, you will refer the **5–28** judge to a reported case from which you derive authority for a proposition that you are advancing. There is a standard operating procedure in those circumstances, which Chapter 10 describes in detail. Part of that procedure involves offering the judge a summary of the facts of the case. If the judge takes you up on the offer, you will be expected to provide a short and accurate synopsis. Rather than make it up on the spot, you should prepare summaries in advance of the moot.

Your summaries need not be long and should focus on the central facts of each reported decision. Given how familiar you are likely to be with your cited authorities by the time you draft your notes, producing summaries should not be an onerous task. Since you will not know precisely when, or even whether, you will need these notes, it is again best to draft them either at the end of the main body of your notes or on a separate sheet of paper.

## Note the correct form of address for the judge

You may find it useful (as some practising advocates do) to write the proper mode of **5–29** addressing the judge[2] at the beginning of your notes or even at the top of each page. Getting the mode of address wrong is less of a peril in mooting than in practice. A moot judge is

---

[2] Chapter 9 discusses the correct modes of address.

almost always a "My Lady" or a "My Lord", whereas professional advocates often appear within short periods of time in front of judges at different levels of the judicial hierarchy who must be addressed in different ways. Nonetheless, a note of the correct form of address may still provide a useful reminder.

# Media for notes

5–30 Regardless of the style of notes you use, you will not make the best use of them at the moot if they are written on multiple scraps of paper arranged in no particular order. Indeed, there are few surer ways of removing the veneer of professionalism from a mooting performance than to lose time rummaging around among sheaves of paper for the one crumpled page that contains the notes for your next submission.

It is therefore vital that you transfer your notes onto a medium that is neat and user-friendly. There are four obvious candidates. They are arranged below in the order of their popularity in professional practice.

## Counsel's notebooks

5–31 Many, if not most, law students will not have come across a counsel's notebook. Yet those who go on to appear regularly in court will find within a few years of starting practice that their office shelves are littered with them. For the uninitiated, counsel's notebooks are like blue school jotters, only taller. They contain approximately 50 lined pages of A4 that are each perforated on the left-hand side. They are sold by most stationers.

There are many advantages to writing your notes for submissions in counsel's notebooks. They are bound, which means that you will not have to juggle numerous loose pieces of paper. They are flexible because the perforations allow you to remove pages easily. By virtue of their shape and suppleness, they are also easy to handle when you are on your feet; you do not, for example, need a lectern to use them.

## Ring binders

5–32 The second most prevalent medium for notes in the legal profession is probably the ring binder. The notes themselves are on hole-punched sheets of A4, either in manuscript or typed-up. A few blank sheets are often inserted at the end of the file for notes made during the hearing.

Ring binders have many of the attributes of counsel's notebooks: they keep all of your notes together in one place; they allow you to remove pages; and they look smart. They have the additional benefit that you can insert pages and dividers. The one drawback with ring binders is that they are tricky to manhandle without a lectern. If this is the medium that you choose for your notes and you discover that your moot courtroom is not equipped with a lectern, you are probably best advised to lie the ring binder flat on the table in front of you as you speak. You may, as a result, be forced to look down rather more often than you would wish.

# Loose sheets of paper

This is the medium that most mooters use for their notes. Some type them up; most write **5–33** them in manuscript. Although loose sheets are likely to be the most cost-effective and readily available option for students, this is probably a case of "you get what you pay for". If your notes are of the fuller variety, you may be dealing with 10 sheets or more, together, of course, with the moot problem and copies of each of the cited authorities. It is no small task to marshal such a volume of paper when you are addressing a judge. You can make that task slightly easier if you colour code your notes. You might, for example, write your prepared submissions on ordinary white paper, but have summaries of your authorities written out on blue paper. You should also make sure that all of the pages are numbered.

Nonetheless, with all of this foolscap flying around, accidents can happen. The dangers of a mishap can be reduced by stapling the loose sheets together. But it is never easy to deal elegantly with a stapled bundle of papers, particularly if you have to move backwards and forwards through it as you deal with the judge's interventions.

# Cards

The great virtue of cards and the primary reason why they are so prevalent amongst debaters **5–34** and best men, is that they are small. They can consequently be held relatively high, enabling speakers to lift their heads and project their voices forward. What is an undoubted strength in the debating chamber and at wedding receptions is, however, something of a liability in moot courtrooms. Cards simply do not provide sufficient space for the notes that most mooters need. For those who prefer to rely on fairly full notes, the problem is especially acute. They would almost certainly find themselves clutching a pack of cards thick enough to play poker with.

It is only fair to admit that some mooters are able to use cards very effectively. You will struggle, however, to find any practising advocate who writes his or her notes for oral submissions on cards. Unless you are already comfortable and confident using cards, on this issue you should probably trust the professionals.

# Summary

The importance of drafting effective notes for your oral submissions cannot be over- **5–35** estimated. Good notes will provide you with the prompts that you need at the time when you need them, they will act as a flexible reference and they will engender in you the confidence that you require to engage effectively with the judge. Poor notes, by contrast, will be a hindrance to effective communication with the judge and an impediment to winning the moot.

This chapter has taken an in-depth look at this relatively controversial topic. In particular, it has:

- Explained the functions that notes perform.

- Described the various styles of notes.

- Suggested how to improve the effectiveness of your notes.

- Identified the principal media for notes.

- Emphasised that it is the way in which notes are used that ultimately counts.

# 6 Authorities and bundles

During your oral submissions, you will take the judge through the authorities on which your **6-1** team relies to support its arguments. You and the judge therefore need to have hard copies of your chosen reported cases, textbooks and articles. Some seats of learning are happy to produce these for the judge (whether in book or document form). But many academic institutions are not so generous. It is therefore usually up to you to ensure that the judge has copies of your authorities.

In comparison with drafting a skeleton argument or producing notes for submissions, the task of preparing copies of your selected authorities is pretty small beer. But get it wrong and you can be left looking decidedly red-faced. You might even say that, for small beer, it is a surprisingly potent brew. The subject accordingly merits a pint-sized chapter of this book.

## Options for presenting authorities

There are two recognised ways of presenting hard copies of your authorities to the judge. **6-2** The first, and most common, is to hand up each authority during your oral submissions just before you begin to speak about it. The second is to provide the judge with a "bundle" that contains in one bound file copies of all of the authorities on which your team relies. You can hand the judge's bundle to the moot organiser when you exchange lists of authorities (and skeleton arguments) in advance of the moot or you can give it to the judge at the beginning of your team's oral submissions.

The rules of the mooting competition in which you are involved may dictate which of these methods you use. However, even if you are not required to prepare a bundle, you should give serious consideration to doing so. A well prepared bundle will be an asset in almost every moot. The judge will have all of your authorities in one, easily accessible place rather than spread in some ad hoc way across his desk. You will also avoid having to interrupt the flow of your oral submissions every time you refer to an authority; instead of handing up yet another sheaf of paper, you can simply refer the judge to a tab or page in your bundle.

Regardless of the method that you choose for presenting your authorities to the judge, it is important that you get it right. A sloppy job will distract the judge from what you are trying to say and possibly even confuse him. It will all look rather amateurish.

# How to prepare authorities

**6–3** Preparing copies of your authorities is not rocket science, but it is surprising how many rocket scientists get it horribly wrong. All that it takes is a little attention to detail. But you should not underestimate how important that detail can be.

Do not forget that copying authorities is precisely the sort of task that you will be asked to do as a junior lawyer. And there are plenty of senior lawyers, possibly even your future bosses, who take the view that trainees and pupils who cannot copy authorities properly are not to be trusted with more challenging, and consequently more interesting, work.

Set out below is a short guide to preparing authorities accurately and professionally. It assumes that you will make your copies either by printing them off from one of the online databases or by photocopying bound volumes of law reports.

## Do not leave it too late

**6–4** This is the golden rule. If you wait until the last minute before running off copies of your authorities for the judge, you multiply your chances of coming a cropper. The nightmare scenario is that you find that the only working computer terminal or photocopier in the law library is occupied (by someone other than your mooting partner) and that you are unable to make any copies at all. Even if you avoid that apocalypse, by leaving it late, you are very likely to be rushed—never the ideal circumstances in which to do a job that requires attention to detail. You will also be carrying out this mundane task at a time when you should be doing far more important things, such as practising your oral submissions.

There should be no need for this sort of last-ditch panic. Most mooting competitions require the participants to exchange lists of authorities at least 24 hours before the moot begins. You should therefore know well in advance of the moot which authorities you have to produce for the judge.

## Copy the correct version of case reports

**6–5** As we saw in Chapter 4 in the context of citing authorities in skeleton arguments, the same case often appears in more than one series of law reports. Make sure that the version you copy for the judge is the same as the one that you intend to refer to at the moot and that appears in your team's list of authorities and skeleton argument (if you have served one). If you provide the judge with a copy of a different version, you can guarantee confusion all round as you refer to page or paragraph numbers that do not correspond to those in the document that the judge has in front of him.

## Make unabridged copies of case reports

**6–6** It not uncommonly happens that mooters copy only those pages of case reports to which they actually intend to refer in the course of their oral submissions. The result can sometimes be that 50-page-plus case reports are reduced to as little as two sheets of A4. The motivation for this reductivist tendency is often a laudable desire to protect the environment. But being a Friend of the Earth is unlikely to make you a friend of the judge. He will usually want to see the entire report so that he can place the passages on which you rely in their proper context and make up his own mind about their relevance. As a general rule, you should therefore present the judge with a copy of the complete report.

Some common sense must be applied, however. You may, for example, wish to refer to a particularly lengthy case report, much of which comprises the arguments of counsel and the judgments of a lower court. In those circumstances, it will usually be perfectly appropriate to hand up a truncated version. Precisely what goes in to that version will differ in each case, although it should always include the headnote and will almost always include complete copies of all of the judgments of the senior court. That might be the approach that you would take if you wished to rely, for instance, on *White v Jones* [1995] 2 AC 207, one of the leading English authorities on duty of care in negligence. The full report is 88 pages long, but the headnote and judgments of the House of Lords run to a "mere" 47 pages.

## Copy sufficient pages of textbooks to provide context

A different approach is required when you copy extracts from textbooks. No mooter is going **6–7** to attempt to copy hundreds of pages in order to refer to just one. But where should you draw the line? As a general rule, you should copy sufficient pages to give the judge a flavour of the context of the passage on which you rely. In most cases, that will be more than just the page containing your passage, but probably not more than three or four pages in total. Make sure that you also include as the first page of the authority a copy of the title page of the textbook so that the judge can see which book you are referring to and the date of publication.

## Ensure that your copies are complete

It is not much use copying an authority if the critical passage is completely or partially **6–8** missing. Once you have run off a copy of an authority, you should therefore get into the habit of reviewing it. Ensure, in particular, that no page is missing (some photocopiers have a nasty habit of skipping pages), that the entirety of each page has been copied (some printers and photocopiers have a nasty habit of cutting off the bottoms, tops or sides of pages) and that every page is in the correct order (some mooters have a nasty habit of inadvertently re-ordering case reports).

## Make your copies one-for-one

Do not produce copies of authorities on which the text is so small that it is virtually **6–9** illegible to anyone with less than 20/20 vision. If anything, you should veer towards magnifying the text. Save for particularly lengthy case reports, when the practice can be justified, you should also avoid producing double-sided copies or copying two pages from the original onto each sheet of the copy.

## Do not mark the copies

**6–10**   Best practice is to present the judge with clean copies of your authorities. If he wants to mark them in some way, he will do so himself prior to or during the moot. It is accordingly advisable to hand up authorities already highlighted in numerous inks. On no account should you hand up authorities with manuscript annotations.

## Make sufficient copies

**6–11**   It is not unknown for mooters to find themselves clutching a copy of an authority to which they are about to refer, but with none to give to the judge. Very often, the only remedy in this unfortunate situation is for the mooter to hand up his own copy. It can then become very difficult to steer the judge in the direction of the relevant passages.

   In order to avoid this fate, you should prepare two copies of each of your authorities: one for yourself and one for the judge. If you handed in a bundle for the judge in advance of the moot, do not assume that he will bring it with him. Prepare a spare copy and take it with you to the moot.

## Fasten your copies

**6–12**   If you are handing up authorities one-by-one, each copy that you present should be individually fastened, preferably with a staple. If the authority is too long to be stapled, fasten it in some other way, for example with a bulldog clip or with one of those pieces of string with metal-covered ends (technically known as treasury tags). You should avoid paper clips as they tend not to keep documents securely fastened for long. Even paper clips are better than nothing, however.

   If you are providing a bundle, your authorities will automatically be securely fastened. You should insert them into the bundle in loose-leaf form. If they are stapled together, the judge will probably have to take them out of the bundle in order to read them. Some of the benefit of using a bundle will then be lost.

## A final flip through

**6–13**   When you have followed all of this advice and you have in front of you a neat stack or bundle of authorities, flick through them one last time. Make sure that every authority is present and correct, and arranged in the order that you will require it at the moot.

## Additional considerations specific to bundles

**6–14**   It will not surprise you to learn that professional lawyers are subject to detailed rules about the preparation and contents of bundles, as well as, of course, strict deadlines by which they must be submitted to the court.[1] As a mooter, you will not be so constrained. Nonetheless,

---

[1] For examples of the rules that apply in England, see paragraphs 3.1 to 3.10 of the Practice Direction to Part 39 of the CPR and Appendix 2 of the Chancery Guide.

whether you prepare a bundle on your own initiative or because you are bound (as it were) by the competition rules, there are a few things that you should know about how to do it.

## Choice of binding

You have a number of options. Which one you choose will probably come down to personal **6–15** preference and the resources at your disposal. All that really matters is that the pages are securely contained, but sufficiently accessible to enable the judge to make margin notes on the documents. Comb binding (which employs pieces of plastic with "teeth") and wire spiral binding are accordingly both perfectly good techniques, although you will need access to the necessary equipment. Treasury tags are also fine.

Best of all is a ring binder. It looks professional and is user-friendly. You should also be able to employ ring binders more than once (which probably makes them re-user-friendly) as judges will happily return bundles of authorities to the competitors if so requested.

## Labels

The judge will want to see at a glance which team's bundle he has in front of him. You **6–16** should therefore attach an identifying label to the spine or the front of the bundle or both.

## Contents

It is all too easy to produce a bundle that looks presentable on the outside, but is a muddled **6–17** mess on the inside. In order to ensure that your bundles do not fall into that trap, take the following steps:

- **Arrange the contents in a logical order**
  Ideally, your authorities should appear in the bundle in the order that your team intends to refer to them during your oral submissions. If, as some mooters do, you insert a copy of your skeleton argument in the bundle, put it at the front.

- **Clearly separate each authority**
  Every authority in the bundle should be placed behind a divider or separated in some other way (such as by coloured "post-it" notes). Otherwise, the judge will have to flick through the entire bundle each time that he has to locate an authority.

- **Draft an index**
  Insert an index at the beginning of the bundle. It should include the name of the moot problem and list the authorities in the order in which they appear in the bundle. Each authority should be given its full citation.

- **Consider paginating the bundle**
  If your bundle is not too long, you should consider inserting sequential numbers in manuscript at the bottom of each page. Whilst by no means necessary, pagination can speed up references to your authorities during oral submissions. Rather than pointing the judge to a tab in the bundle and then the internal page number of the authority, you can simply ask him to *"turn to page* [X]".

- **Hole-punch carefully**
  If the preparation of your bundle involves hole punching, make sure that you insert the holes in the same place on each page. Deviation from this practice tends to leave the edges of your authorities with the appearance of badly folded newspapers.

## Summary

**6–18** Careful preparation of your authorities will pay dividends. Not only will moot judges follow your submissions with greater ease, they will also be impressed by the organisational and presentational skills that you have displayed.

This short chapter has explained how you can produce those desired effects. It has, in particular:

- Explained how to prepare copies of authorities for judges that are error-free and user-friendly.

- Described how to produce polished and well organised bundles of authorities.

# 7 Practising oral submissions

Practising your oral submissions is a vital part of preparing for moots. The more that you  **7–1**
practise, and the more effective your practising is, the more polished and persuasive your
submissions will be. You should therefore make sure that you carve out sufficient time to
practise your submissions, however frenetic the build-up to the moot may be.

This short chapter is divided into two parts: the first identifies the objectives of practising
submissions; the second provides a number of suggestions for how to go about it.

## Objectives of practice

Most mooters practise their oral submissions at least once before each moot. But if your  **7–2**
practice regimen is limited to a quick read through your notes on the morning of the moot,
you will not derive all of the benefits that you should from this stage of preparation. The key
objectives of practising your oral submissions are outlined below. Bear them in mind when
you practise.

### Time your submissions

You need to know how long your prepared submissions will last so that you can make sure  **7–3**
that what you plan to say neither exceeds your allotted speaking time nor leaves valuable
time unutilised. You should therefore time your submissions when you practise them,
preferably more than once so that you can check for consistency.

Given that your speaking time at the moot is likely to be relatively short, you must time
your submissions accurately. If possible, use a clock that displays seconds or, better still, a
stopwatch. You should also time yourself in circumstances that replicate actual mooting
conditions. The following tips should help to give you a reasonable estimate of how long
your oral submissions will actually last:

- **Practise with your papers**
  You should practise using all of the papers that you will have to marshal at the moot.
  You will lose time whenever you move from one sheet of paper to another. Build that
  delay into your timing.

- **Take account of time lost when you refer to authorities**

  You will also lose time whenever you refer the judge to one of your authorities. However dexterous your judge may be, he will inevitably need a few seconds to find the right page and paragraph. You will have to halt your submissions while he does so. Factor this hiatus into your timing.

- **Allow time for the judge's questions (if necessary)**

  The rules of the mooting competition will stipulate whether or not the clock stops running when the judge asks questions. If it does not, you will need to allow sufficient time in your oral submissions, perhaps two or three minutes, for dealing with judicial interventions.

After timing your submissions, you may find it helpful to record in your notes a few key "milestones" that you can then use during the moot to gauge the pace of your delivery. For example, you might mark the point in your notes (perhaps by making a small notation in the margin) when you expect to have reached the halfway point in your allotted speaking time. If, as you are delivering your oral submissions at the moot, you pass this point sooner than expected, you will know to slow down. If it takes you longer to get to your marker than it did when you were practising, you will need to increase your pace or skip a point.

## Polish your notes

7–4 Practising your submissions will enable you to improve your notes. For example, if you have drafted a full speech, practising it should highlight any clumsy phraseology. You can then amend it. If you have drafted more truncated notes, running through your submissions should tell you whether they provide the prompts that you need in order to remember the points that you wish to make. Any notes that are insufficient for that purpose can be supplemented accordingly.

## Familiarise yourself with your submissions

7–5 Whether you are relying on a full written speech or minimal notes, practising your submissions will help you to remember them. That is not to say that you should set out to memorise your oral submissions word-for-word, although you may find that this happens naturally as you practise them. It is rather that you want to have as much of your submissions as possible in your head so that you are not overly tied to the page when you speak and can make regular eye contact with the judge. At the very least, practising your submissions will familiarise you with your notes and enable you to find specific information in a hurry.

## Improve your delivery

7–6 Practising your oral submissions should improve your delivery in a number of ways. In the first place, as you become more familiar with your submissions, you should be able to speak with a more natural voice. Repeated practice should also help you to identify any potentially distracting verbal habits or physical mannerisms. Some people are prone, for example, to repeating particular words without realising it; the word "basically" is a common offender. Others have a tendency to clear their throats with unnatural regularity. Yet others play with their earlobes or twiddle pens in their fingers. All of these idiosyncracies can be spotted and ironed out as you practise your submissions.

## Build your confidence

The more that you practise your submissions, the more confident you are likely to feel at the moot. You will be more conversant with your notes and will therefore be less worried about losing your place. You will know your arguments better too and should consequently feel more able to defend them. **7–7**

## How to practise

You can practise your submissions in a variety of ways. Some of the most common and effective are described below. But first, a few general observations. For, whichever practice methods you employ, you should aim to get the most out of them. You are more likely to do so if you keep the following advice at the forefront of your mind: **7–8**

- **Practice should be authentic**
  Most mooters practise their submissions at home. There is nothing wrong with that. But if you can run through your speech at least once in the actual moot courtroom or a room just like it, the experience will be considerably more authentic and, consequently, more helpful, particularly for the novice mooter. Maximising authenticity also requires you to speak in the body position that you will adopt at the moot. Almost invariably, you will have to deliver your oral submissions standing up. So practise them in that position, and not lounging on the sofa with a drink in your hand.

- **Force yourself to look up at regular intervals**
  The more eye contact that you can have with the judge, the more effective your oral submissions are likely to be. You should therefore use your practice sessions to test how often you can lift your eyes from the page. If you lose your place in your notes now and again, it does not matter. Try to "ad lib" a few sentences. You may even prefer the "off the cuff" submission to your prepared material. If you are struggling to look up regularly, perhaps because you are working from a full written speech, memorise a few key passages and practise delivering them with your head held high.

- **Focus on the substance of your submissions as well as the delivery**
  Even though you will be practising your submissions relatively close to the moot (most likely, the night before or the morning of) it is not too late to tinker with the substance of your arguments. As you practise, you should therefore keep a weather eye on the persuasiveness of what you are saying. You may well find one or two points that looked convincing on paper, but sound hollow when you express them out loud.

With these generic points in mind, you are ready to start practising. Five different practice methods are described in the paragraphs that follow. Use as many of them as you can as often as you are able. It is very hard to practise too much.

## Practising out loud on your own

7–9   This is probably most people's idea of practising their submissions. It involves running through your oral submissions in the speaking voice that you will adopt at the moot. You may well feel quite self-conscious when you practise in this way, even if you lock yourself in your bedroom and stay well out of earshot of anyone else. But it is hugely valuable, particularly for timing your submissions, committing them to memory and working on your delivery.

Another helpful feature of speaking out loud is that it will accustom you to the sound of your own voice. Many law students are only too familiar with (and enamoured of) the lilt and cadence of their own voices. But there are others who have not had the benefit of listening to themselves speaking regularly in public. This form of practice will acquaint you with how you sound.

## Practising in front of a mirror

7–10   You can take practising out loud a step further by standing in front of a mirror while you speak. What you will gain from this, apparently narcissistic, exercise is a very clear idea of whether you know your submissions well enough to make frequent eye contact with the judge. If you can look yourself steadily in the eyes for long periods, you should be able to do the same thing to the judge.

Practising your submissions in front of a mirror can also highlight mannerisms that might not otherwise be apparent to you. You are likely to benefit most if you can use a full-length mirror that allows you to watch your whole body as you speak.

## Practising in front of someone else

7–11   Ideally, you should practise your oral submissions for each moot at least once in front of someone else, preferably your mooting partner (if you have one). This form of practice will provide an objective assessment of your performance. An observer should be able to give you valuable feedback about the persuasiveness of your arguments and will be better than you at spotting any distracting physical or verbal habits.

If possible, your audience should not be passive, but should play the part of the judge and intervene with questions of the type that the judge might ask at the moot. Such an audience will give you an opportunity to practise responding to judicial interventions and, in the process, to skip around your notes. You will then not only become more familiar with your notes, you will also have a more accurate sense of how long your submissions are likely to last.

## Practising with audio tapes and video recorders

7–12   If you have access to audio or video equipment, you may learn a great deal from recording your performance for posterity. Listening to yourself on tape can be quite a disconcerting experience; you may think that you have the dulcet tones of Sean Connery, but the tape might reveal that you sound more like David Beckham. The experience can be useful, however, particularly as it will ruthlessly highlight your "ums" and "errs", as well as any words and phrases that you employ with irritating regularity.

If listening to your voice on audio tape is tough, seeing yourself on video is downright disturbing. But if you can deal with the cringe factor, watching yourself on screen can be hugely enlightening. It will not only provide you with a good appreciation of what you look and sound like on your feet, it should also give a sense of how engaging you are as a speaker. You will see very quickly whether you look as though you are reading a speech and you will spot any problems with your stance and delivery. Of course, you may also discover that you appear far more accomplished than you actually felt while the tape was rolling. That realisation will provide a welcome confidence boost.

## Practising in silence

By far the easiest way of practising your submissions is to go over them in your head. You **7–13** might, for example, carry a copy of your notes around with you, read a line or two when you have a moment and then to try to continue the submission without looking at your notes. This form of practice is perhaps best used for committing oral submissions to memory and familiarising yourself with the lay-out of your notes.

Another useful exercise is to think about the interventions that the judge might make during your oral submissions. The more that you can play around with ideas in your head, the more likely you are to anticipate the focus of the judge's questions and the more opportunity you will have to consider how you might answer them.

The beauty of practising submissions in silence is that you can do it virtually anywhere and at almost any time. You can even do it on public transport. Just make sure that you do not move your lips too much or your fellow travellers may start to question your sanity.

## Summary

You should practise your submissions before a moot as thoroughly and as often as possible. **7–14** This chapter should help you to do so. It has, in particular:

- Outlined the objectives of practising oral submissions.

- Described the different ways of practising submissions effectively.

# Appearing

*"One junior rose—with eyeballs tense,*
*And swollen frontal veins:*
*To all his powers of eloquence*
*He gave the fullest reins."*

W S Gilbert (1836–1911)

# 8 Getting your bearings

For the uninitiated, a moot courtroom must seem a bit like a foreign country. It has a **8–1**
distinctive geography, it has its own set of customs and it is populated by not altogether
friendly natives. If you are about to appear in your first moot, it will therefore pay dividends
to spend some time learning about your destination before you leave home.

This short chapter aims to provide your preparatory reading. It will familiarise you with
the moot courtroom, explain what you ought to pack and tell you when you should travel to
the moot. It will even provide advice on coping with nerves, the mooter's equivalent of
"Delhi belly". Think of this chapter, therefore, as a *Lonely Planet* guide for mooters.

## Lay-out of moot courtrooms

Moot courtrooms vary tremendously from institution to institution. The grander examples **8–2**
are almost indistinguishable from real courts, coming fully equipped with witness stands, jury
boxes and microphones. The majority of moot courtrooms are rather less imposing,
however, often being nothing more than working classrooms with the furniture moved
around.

Whether grand or humble, moot courtrooms mimic real courts in their lay-out. As figures
8.1 and 8.2 illustrate, the standard configuration of a moot court is slightly different in
England and Scotland.

These standard lay-outs accommodate all of the protagonists in a moot: the judge (or
judges), the mooters and the moot court clerk, as well as the audience. The typical seating
arrangements for each are discussed in more detail below.

### Judge

The moot judge sits at the front of the moot courtroom at the "bench". In the better- **8–5**
appointed moot courtrooms, the bench consists of a fixed wooden desk with sufficient space
to accommodate up to three judges sitting line abreast. Very often, this desk is on a raised
platform, enabling the judges to look down from their lofty perch on the mooters below. In
more modest moot courtrooms, the bench is no more than a table or two sitting at the same
level as the rest of the furniture.

**Figure 8.1: Lay-out of English moot courtroom**

8–3

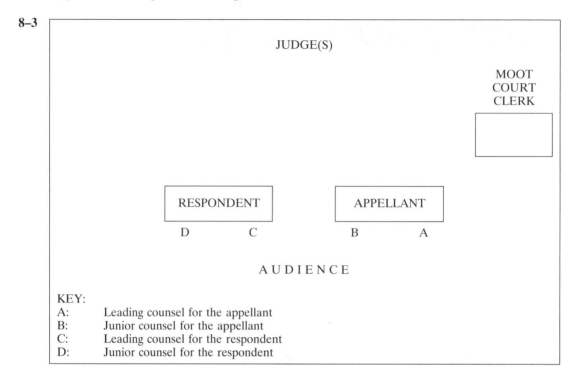

KEY:
A:      Leading counsel for the appellant
B:      Junior counsel for the appellant
C:      Leading counsel for the respondent
D:      Junior counsel for the respondent

**Figure 8.2: Lay-out of Scottish moot courtroom**

8–4

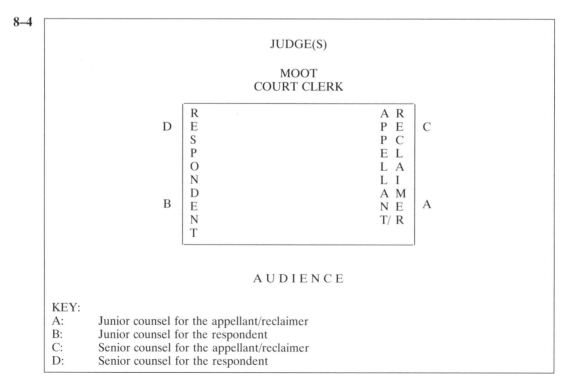

KEY:
A:      Junior counsel for the appellant/reclaimer
B:      Junior counsel for the respondent
C:      Senior counsel for the appellant/reclaimer
D:      Senior counsel for the respondent

## Mooters

Looking from the back of the moot courtroom, the mooters appearing for the appellant sit **8–6** on the right and those for the respondent sit on the left. From the perspective of the bench, counsel for the appellant are therefore on the left and counsel for the respondent on the right. As figures 8.1 and 8.2 show, whereas in England and Wales each team generally sits at its own table facing forward, in Scotland there is usually one central table at which both teams sit opposite each other.

Lecterns are often provided for the mooters to use. Occasionally, there is a single, free-standing lectern from which the mooters make their submissions in turn. More commonly, one or two portable lecterns are placed on the table or tables at which the mooters sit during the moot. Often, there are more mooters than lecterns. In that event, when each mooter finishes speaking, he must pass the lectern to the next mooter to address the court.

## Moot court clerk

Not every mooting competition employs a moot court clerk. When they are used, however, **8–7** they either sit directly in front of the judge, if the judge is seated on a raised dais, or slightly to one side of the bench. The moot court clerk is usually provided with a desk on which to rest papers and any equipment for timing the mooters' submissions.

## Audience

The "public gallery" is normally situated at the back of the moot courtroom, the spectators **8–8** sitting in rows of chairs that start a few feet behind the mooters.

## What to take to the moot (and what not to take)

Mooters, like junior practitioners, must bring to court a considerable amount of parapher- **8–9** nalia. In the heated build-up to a moot, it is all too easy to forget something. It is therefore worth compiling a list and gathering together everything on it before you leave home.

Set out below is a checklist of the items that every mooter should normally take to each moot. Those marked with an asterisk are essential; the remainder are a matter of personal preference.

- **One copy of the moot problem***
- **The notes that you have drafted for your oral submissions***
- **Two copies of any skeleton argument that you have drafted***
  One copy is for you and the other is for the judge in case he did not receive your skeleton argument before the moot or forgot to bring it along. There is, of course, no

need for both you and your mooting partner to bring a spare copy of your skeleton for the judge.

- **Two copies of each authority to which you will refer during your oral submissions\***
  Again, one of these copies is for your use during the moot and the other is for the judge. It is worth taking a spare copy for the judge even if you have provided a bundle of authorities in advance of the moot because there is always a risk that the judge has not received it or has (perish the thought) mislaid it.

- **One copy of each authority on which your opponents rely\***
  It is for your opponents to ensure that the judge has copies of their authorities. There is consequently no need for you to come armed with spares.

- **One copy of your opponents' skeleton argument\***

- **A pen\***

- **A second pen**
  Just in case your first pen packs up during the moot.

- **A highlighter**
  Highlighters are very handy for marking authorities, particularly those passages on which your opponents rely or that the judge identifies as important.

- **Spare sheets of paper for making notes during the moot[1]**

- **"Post-it" notes**
  "Post-it" notes are invaluable for identifying particular documents or parts of documents. They are also useful as repositories of short notes to your mooting partner.

With all of this clobber to carry, it will be a wonder if you have room in your bag for anything else. If you do, avoid the temptation to pack a good luck charm and display it on your table in the moot courtroom. Battered teddy bears and pink gonks may be *de rigueur* on *University Challenge*, but they are incompatible with the air of confident professionalism that you are endeavouring to create at a moot. If you really must bring a furry friend, keep him or her (or it) well away from public view.

## Travelling to the moot

8–10   Even if you do not have far to travel, you should always set out in time to arrive at the moot court at least 15 minutes before the moot is due to begin. If you cut your journey too fine, you are likely to arrive flushed, flustered and a bag of nerves.

Arriving in good time for the moot does not mean that you are obliged to wait for an eternity outside the moot courtroom twiddling your thumbs or engaging in that rather false bonhomie that often precedes moots, exams and other such occasions. You may wish to do

---

[1] An alternative to having separate sheets of paper is to create space within your notes. Chapter 5 discusses the format of notes in detail.

so, of course. You may also wish to scope out the moot courtroom and make yourself at home. But if you do not, an alternative is to get yourself to within a short distance of the moot court door, possibly a nearby classroom, and remain there until a few minutes before the moot is scheduled to begin. If you have a mooting partner, the two of you can arrange to meet at this neutral location and use the period before the moot starts to run over your oral submissions one last time.

# Coping with nerves

Pre-moot nerves can be pretty unpleasant. Different people are affected in different ways, of **8–11** course, but the classic symptoms are sweaty palms, loss of appetite, wobbles in the lower intestines, shaky hands and uncontrollable yawns. It is almost as though you are ill.

If you are a sufferer, take heart from the fact that your nerves will naturally diminish as your mooting experience grows. They may also disappear altogether whenever you stand up at a moot to begin your oral submissions. In the meantime, however, there are at least two things that you can do to reduce your anxiety. These suggestions are not panaceas. But then your aim is not to become a nerveless automaton. A touch of pre-moot nerves is a healthy indication that adrenaline is pumping through your body. Adrenaline will increase your energy levels, sharpen your wits and improve your performance at the moot.

## Prepare thoroughly

At the heart of most people's nervousness about mooting is a fear of the unexpected, particularly of the questions that the judge will ask. If you want to reduce your nerves, you should therefore minimise the unknown element. The primary unknown for most mooters is the law. So you must research the law as thoroughly as you can for each moot. The better that you understand the legal issues that the moot problem raises, the less likely it is that the judge will ask you a question that you cannot answer.[2]

If you are a novice mooter, part of the uncertainty of mooting is not knowing what a moot court looks like. Reading this chapter should give you an idea, but there is no substitute for paying a visit to the room that will be your moot court. Familiarise yourself with its lay-out and, if you can, try the acoustics at the spot from which you will speak.

## Keep a sense of perspective

Although you might feel as if you are suffering from the world's worst case of moot-induced nervous paralysis, you are actually going through nothing more than countless others have experienced before you and will experience after you. Indeed, most practising advocates regularly suffer from nerves. And they, at least, have the excuse of representing real clients whose liberty and livelihoods may be at stake.

---

[2] Chapter 11 provides detailed guidance on anticipating judicial interventions.

You will not be expected to scale the heights of oratorical brilliance in the course of your oral submissions. If you demonstrate competence, show a good understanding of the moot problem and the relevant law, and articulate your points comprehensibly and clearly, you will impress the judge and the audience.

## Summary

**8–12** If mooters are to look the part in the moot courtroom, they must know what to expect when they arrive at the moot. They must also come properly equipped, mentally as well as physically. This chapter has sought to give you the guidance that you need in this regard. In particular, it has:

- Described the lay-out of a typical moot courtroom.

- Identified what to bring to a moot.

- Explained how to cope with nerves.

# 9 Moot court etiquette

According to George Bernard Shaw, *"We don't bother much about dress and manners in* **9–1** *England, because as a nation we don't dress well and we've no manners."*[1] Clearly, GBS never mooted. Had he done so, he would have realised that, in English and Scottish moot courtrooms at least, etiquette is highly valued.

The importance accorded to etiquette in mooting is largely a reflection of its central role in creating a civilised and professional environment. Moots are not university union-style debates, but mock court hearings. They must accordingly assume some of the order and solemnity of real legal proceedings. The rules of etiquette help to foster the requisite atmosphere.

The purpose of this chapter is to steer you through the minefield of moot court etiquette. It will, amongst other things, explain what you should wear, identify the proper forms of address for judges and fellow mooters, and provide guidance on modern mooting manners. If the last chapter was a *Lonely Planet* guide for mooters, this chapter is a mooters' *Debrett's*.

## Dress

There are not too many professions that can claim that what they wear to work is a source of **9–2** heated public debate, but the British legal profession is one of them. In fact, such is the perceived importance of public attitudes to court dress that barely a year seems to go by without the publication of yet another report on the subject.

Mooters may only rarely wear wigs (the source of most of the controversy surrounding what British lawyers wear), but they are not immune from this obsession with matters sartorial. In particular, some take exception to having to dress up in business attire in order to moot. Before examining exactly what it is that mooters ought to wear, it is therefore worth considering why you should leave your Levi 501s at home when you moot.

### Why have a dress code?

In an age so informal that the President of the United States can greet the Prime Minister of **9–3** the United Kingdom with the words, "Yo, Blair!", you might well wonder what useful purpose can be served by requiring mooters to don formal dress. There are, in fact, a hatful

---

[1] *George Bernard Shaw, You Never Can Tell, Act I.*

of reasons (or, as George W Bush might prefer it, a Stetson-full). Some of them are set out below:

- **You will look professional**

  Mooting is modelled on professional practice. The law is one of those professions that employ conservative dress. Professional advocates therefore wear business attire. Mooters should too.

- **You will feel professional**

  Dressing up will make you feel the part. If you feel like a professional advocate, you are more likely to act like one.

- **Your dress will not be a distraction**

  If you are wearing much the same attire as every other mooter, judges will find it easier to concentrate on what you are saying and will not be distracted by how you look. By contrast, they will struggle to follow your submissions if you appear before them in a tee-shirt emblazoned with the latest legend from French Connection ("*I love mcok courts*", perhaps?).

- **You will impress the judge**

  Dressing properly will create a strong first impression on the judge. Some moot judges are very particular about advocates' dress and will mark down any mooter who does not meet the required standard. The most pernickety judges in this regard are often those who are members of the judiciary in real life. Their attitude may be partly explained by their keener awareness of the need for advocates to show respect to the court. But they also doubtless appreciate, from many years of sitting in court, that an untidy advocate all too often produces an untidy argument.

- **It will accustom you to wearing suits**

  Some students feel uncomfortable and self-conscious wearing suits. As an aspiring lawyer, you need to get over this affliction. Even with the arrival of more casual dress codes in many law firms, you will still have to wear a suit for job interviews and for the bulk of your week once you start work.

## What you should wear

**9–4**   In deciding what to wear to a moot, you should first check the rules of your mooting competition. They may incorporate a dress code. In the absence of specific guidance from the rules, you should assume that you are required to wear business attire or the nearest thing to it that you can manage. No-one will expect you to buy a suit especially for a moot, but you will be expected to dress smartly (or, as the English Bar Council's guidance puts it, "decorously"[2]). For the avoidance of doubt, a short guide is provided below.

*Men*

**9–5**   - A two- or three-piece suit, preferably in navy, charcoal grey or black. Failing that, a pair of smart trousers in a dark colour or khaki, and a jacket.

---

[2] Paragraph 5.13 of the Bar Council's Written Standards for Professional Work.

- A collared shirt, ideally in white or a mild shade of a neutral colour like blue, pink or purple. Conservative patterns, such as thin stripes, are acceptable too.
- A tie. Avoid anything too garish. The judge should not be treated to one of your hilarious ties from the Homer Simpson neckwear collection.
- A clean pair of smart shoes. You will ruin the effect of your elegant suit if you turn up at the moot in a scruffy pair of "brothel creepers".

### Women

- A skirt- or trouser-suit, preferably in black, navy or dark grey. If you do not own a **9–6** suit, wear a skirt or a pair of trousers with a jacket. Skirts should be at least knee-length.
- A business-style shirt. The same principles apply to colours and patterns for women's shirts as to men's.
- A pair of smart shoes. Heels are fine, but remember that you are going to have to stand for quite long periods while you make your oral submissions. You should probably therefore leave the six-inch stilettos at home.

## Wearing gowns

In order to inject greater realism into the proceedings, some mooting competitions require **9–7** the competitors to wear gowns. Gowns are not the most user-friendly garments. Wear one that is too small and you run the risk of looking like Alice in Wonderland after drinking the potion that made her grow. An even worse fate awaits if your gown is too large. It will quickly start to slip from your shoulders and down your back, and the commodious sleeves will dangle precariously from your arms, getting in the way when you handle your papers. A super-sized gown may also lodge itself under your chair when you sit down, thereby guaranteeing an embarrassing commotion when you try to stand up again. Given the inconvenience that an ill-fitting gown can cause, if you are able to choose one to wear at the moot, it is worth taking care to ensure that it actually fits.

## When does the dress code apply?

Unless you are told otherwise, the dress code applies whenever you are in the moot **9–8** courtroom and not just when you are on your feet making submissions to the judge. You should not therefore arrive at the moot court in trainers and proceed to change into a smarter pair of shoes when one of your opponents is addressing the court. Nor should you take off your jacket or loosen your tie once you have finished your speech. You should also maintain your standard of dress when you return to the moot courtroom to receive the judge's verdict (however refreshing any interval drinks may have been).

## Forms of address

Few matters of moot court etiquette cause more trouble than the modes of address that **9–9** mooters are supposed to adopt when they refer to judges or their fellow advocates. The required forms of address are old-fashioned and sound odd to the unpractised ear, but you need to master them if you are to avoid looking (and feeling) awkward and inexperienced.

# The moot judge

**9–10**    The British courts employ a plethora of forms of address for judges at different levels of the judicial hierarchy.[3] As a result, junior practitioners sometimes struggle to refer to judges properly, particularly if they appear in quick succession before tribunals that should be addressed in different ways. Thankfully, the task of addressing a moot judge is relatively straightforward because English and Scots law moots invariably take place in courts where all of the judges are addressed in the same way.

Table 9.1 sets out the proper forms of address when the moot court is the House of Lords, the Court of Appeal, the Court of Session or the High Court of Justiciary.

## Table 9.1: Forms of address for the moot judge

**9–11**

| Tribunal | "Direct" form of address | In place of "you" | In place of "your" |
|---|---|---|---|
| Single male judge | "My Lord" | "Your Lordship" | "Your Lordship's" |
| Single female judge | "My Lady" | "Your Ladyship" | "Your Ladyship's" |
| All-male panel of judges | Collectively: "My Lords" <br> Individually: "My Lord" | Collectively: "Your Lordships" <br><br> Individually: "Your Lordship" | Collectively: "Your Lordships'" <br><br> Individually: "Your Lordship's" |
| All-female panel of judges | Collectively: "My Ladies" <br> Individually: "My Lady" | Collectively: "Your Ladyships" <br><br> Individually: "Your Ladyship" | Collectively: "Your Ladyships'" <br><br> Individually: "Your Ladyship's" |
| Mixed sex panel of judges | Collectively: "My Lords" <br> Individually: "My Lord" or "My Lady" as appropriate | Collectively: "Your Lordships" <br><br> Individually: "Your Lordship" or "Your Ladyship" as appropriate | Collectively: "Your Lordships'" <br><br> Individually: "Your Lordship's" or "Your Ladyship's" as appropriate |

**9–12**    As the second column of table 9.1 shows, when addressing the judge directly (in other words, when you would in normal parlance use his or her name), you should employ "My Lord", "My Lady" or the appropriate plural form. For example, you might say as follows:

> *"My Lord, I appear on behalf of the respondent in this appeal"*; or

> *"It is submitted, My Ladies, that the leading case in this area of the law is . . ."*.

As appears from the third and fourth columns of table 9.1, you should never use the pronoun "you" or the possessive adjective "your" when speaking to a judge. Instead, you should employ "Your Lordship/Ladyship", "Your Lordship's/ Ladyship's" or the appropriate plural form. For example, you might say the following:

---

[3] For a comprehensive list of the correct forms of address for members of each level of the judiciary of England and Wales, go to *www.judiciary.gov.uk*.

*"Would Your Ladyships please turn to page two of my skeleton argument?"*; or

*"If I understand Your Lordship's point correctly, . . ."*

There is nothing to stop you from combining more than one form of address in a single sentence. You might therefore say this:

*"My Lord, I would now like to deal with the point that Your Lordship mentioned a moment ago."*

When you first start mooting, you will find these forms of address rather cumbersome and will trip up occasionally. It is particularly easy to place a "My Lord/Lady" where a "Your Lordship/Ladyship" should go, or to make a mistake when the tribunal consists of more than one judge. As you gain in experience, however, you will find that addressing judges correctly becomes almost second nature.

## Judges other than the moot judge

In the course of your oral submissions, you are likely to refer to a number of other judges. **9–13** You will almost certainly mention the fictitious lower court judge who appears in the moot problem and whose decision you are seeking to uphold or overturn. You will also refer to the real life judges whose reported decisions you rely on as authorities.

The titles of some British judges are pronounced differently in court from the way in which they appear in writing. You therefore need to know how to pronounce them properly. Table 9.2 lists some of the most common written titles together with the correct pronunciation.

### Table 9.2: Referring to other judges

**9–14**

| Written | Spoken |
|---|---|
| Smith HHJ | "His/Her Honour Judge Smith" |
| Smith J | "Mr/Mrs Justice Smith" |
| Smith LJ | "Lord/Lady Justice Smith" |
| Smith and Jones LJJ | "Lord/Lady Justices Smith and Jones" |
| Lord Smith of Smithfield | "Lord Smith" |

A final point on referring to other judges: however senior or junior the fictitious lower court judge in the moot problem, when you refer to him or her in your submissions, the convention is to use the phrase "the learned judge". Thus, for example, you might say the following towards the start of your oral submissions:

*"This is an appeal against the decision of Mr Justice Smith. The learned judge held that . . ."*

## Your opponents

**9–15** You are likely to refer to your opponents quite often during your oral submissions. If you are the first mooter to speak, you will need to introduce them. You will also have to mention them whenever you respond to a point that they have made in their written or oral submissions. There are various acceptable formulations for referring to your opponents, most of which are listed below:

- *"My learned friend"*
- *"My learned friend, Mr/Ms [X] (but never use first names)"*
- *"My learned friend opposite"*
- *"Leading/junior counsel for the appellant/respondent"*
- *"Mr/Ms [X]"*

## Your mooting partner

**9–16** Whenever you refer to your mooting partner during your oral submissions, whether in the course of introducing the mooters to the judge or otherwise, you should refer to him or her using one of the following forms:

- *"My learned friend"*
- *"My learned friend, Mr/Ms [X] (but again, do not use first names)"*
- *"My learned junior/leader"*
- *"Mr/Ms [X]"*

# A few points of vocabular etiquette

**9–17** The idiosyncratic vocabulary of the moot court extends beyond forms of address to include a number of phrases that advocates routinely deploy during their oral submissions. All of these phrases are designed to display a suitable deference to the court that the alternatives lack. Three of the more common are briefly discussed below.

## *"In my submission"*

**9–18** As Chapter 4 explained, you should avoid expressing submissions in your skeleton arguments as if they were your own views. Your purpose is not to burden the court with your personal opinions, but to present your client's case in an objective fashion. The same principle applies when you make submissions orally. You should therefore shun phrases such as *"In my opinion, . . ."*, *"It seems to me that . . ."* and *"I think that . . ."*, and use instead the words *"In my submission, . . ."*, *"It is submitted that . . ."*, *"I submit that . . ."* or *"The appellant's/respondent's case is that . . ."*.

## *"I am grateful"*

In the course of your speech, the judge, your mooting partner or your opponents may **9–19** attempt to assist you in some way, for which you need to express thanks. The judge might, for example, indicate that he has already read an authority to which you intend to refer, thereby avoiding the need for you to summarise it for him. Alternatively, your team-mate or one of your opponents might correct an inaccurate case citation that you have just given to the judge. Even if the intervention is essentially unhelpful, you should express your gratitude in one of the following ways:

- *"I am grateful to Your Lordship/Your Ladyship/my learned friend"*
- *"I am grateful"*
- *"I am obliged to Your Lordship/Your Ladyship/my learned friend"*
- *"I am obliged"*

A word of warning, however. Thanking the judge should not descend into Blackadder-esque obsequiousness. If the judge makes a helpful intervention, perhaps by suggesting an argument in your favour that you had not thought of, stick to one of the phrases identified above and avoid any temptation to gush that the judge is "SO right".

## *"With respect"*

There will be occasions during your oral submissions when you have to correct or disagree **9–20** with something that the judge has said. You may, in those circumstances, begin your submission on the subject using the words "with respect". This phrase is perfectly appropriate if expressed with the requisite degree of deference. Without it, however, there is a danger that your "with respect" will sound as though you actually have little or no respect for the judge's view. All the more so, if you choose to employ the words "with the greatest of respect". It is therefore best to keep your use of these expressions to a minimum. Use them only when you are directly contradicting something that the judge has said.

# Standing up and sitting down

There is a recognised protocol governing when mooters should stand in the moot courtroom **9–21** and when they should sit. As ever, this protocol replicates the rules that apply in the courts proper.

You will usually be seated in the moot courtroom before the judge arrives. When he enters the room, you (as well as the audience) should stand. If there is a moot court clerk, he will usually prompt those assembled with the words, "Court rise". Once the judge has reached his seat, he will normally give a small bow of the head before sitting down. You should bow in similar fashion before also sitting down.

Occasionally, the judge will already be seated at the bench when you enter the moot courtroom at the start of the moot. In that event, you should walk to your place and bow. You should then sit down when the judge invites you to do so.

9–22   Unless the judge tells you otherwise, you should always stand when you address him and he addresses you. You should therefore stand when you commence your oral submissions and remain standing throughout your speech, including during any interventions that the judge makes. You should only sit down once you have completed your oral submissions and the judge has indicated that he requires no further assistance from you (which he will often do simply by saying, "Thank you").

It is rare in moots for the judge to invite a mooter to address him during another mooter's speech. If that happens, however, the non-speaking mooter should stand and deal with the judge's point. The mooter who was speaking should meanwhile sit down and wait until the exchange between the judge and the new speaker has finished. The original speaker should then stand to continue his submissions.

Except when the judge addresses a question directly to him, a non-speaking mooter should remain seated. Unlike a debate, you are not entitled to jump to your feet and make a point of information or a point of order. Nor can you holler, "Objection!" *LA Law*-style. If you disagree with what your opponents are saying, make a note of their point. You or your partner can then deal with it in your oral submissions.

9–23   Once both sides have completed their submissions, the judge will normally leave the moot courtroom to consider his verdict. When the judge stands at the end of the moot, you should stand too. Before he moves off, the judge will often bow his head again. If he does, you should follow suit. You should then remain standing until the judge has left the room. If, as sometimes happens, the judge signals that he will remain in the moot court to make his deliberations, the mooters should stand, bow their heads in the judge's direction, and leave the room.

# Good manners

9–24   It would be going too far to suggest that manners maketh the mooter, but bad manners can certainly maketh a very negative impression on the judge. Displaying good manners during a moot involves nothing more than observing common courtesies. Principal among them are these:

- **Turn off your mobile phone**
  There are few things more likely to induce apoplexy in a judge than the ring tone of a mobile phone. Unless you want a crazy judge on your hands as well as the Crazy Frog, turn your mobile off before you enter the moot courtroom and do not switch it back on until after the moot has finished.

- **Do not interrupt the judge**
  If the judge intervenes during your oral submissions, let him complete his point without interruption, even if you see where he is going with his question before he finishes it.

- **Stay silent during your opponents' submissions**
  You may disagree vehemently with what your opponents are saying, but that is no excuse for engaging in theatrical bouts of paper shuffling, coughs, tuts, sharp intakes of breath, titters, yawns, sighs or grunts. Your opponents are entitled to make their points (as are you) without an attendant cacophony of farmyard noise.

- **Pay attention to your partner's submissions**
  There is no need to gaze adoringly on your team-mate as he makes his oral submissions. You are not a Tory politician watching your leader address the party conference. Just make sure that you are (and look as if you are) actively following what your mooting partner is saying. Not only is he entitled to this respect, but it will demonstrate to the judge a modicum of teamwork.[4]

- **Listen attentively to any feedback**
  Few mooters need to be told to pay attention when the judge announces who has won the moot. But you should also listen politely to any feedback that the judge gives, even if you have lost (in fact, particularly if you have lost).

## Summary

However outmoded it might seem, moot court etiquette helps to create a mooting **9–25** experience that closely resembles professional practice. If you are to look the part in that environment, you need to learn the relevant rules and abide by them.

This chapter has described the principal rules of moot court etiquette. In particular, it has:

- Explained how to dress for moots.

- Identified the proper forms of address for judges and mooters.

- Discussed the protocol that determines when to stand and sit during moots.

- Listed the fundamentals of good mooting manners.

---

[4] The role of the non-speaking mooter is discussed in more detail in Chapter 10.

# 10 Oral submissions

10–1 Prepare all you can for a moot (and you should), but winning is ultimately about your performance on the night. However thorough your research, however compelling your skeleton argument and however immaculate your court dress, the judge's decision on the moot largely comes down to your oral submissions: what you say and how you say it.

This chapter explains the skills involved in articulating your arguments to a moot judge. It starts with a *précis* of the basics of speaking in court. It then explains the order of speeches at a moot before examining the constituent elements of a typical mooting speech, from opening to concluding remarks. After providing a number of tips for delivering and timing oral submissions, this chapter ends with some advice on how to behave when you are not speaking. The one conscious omission from this chapter is judicial interventions, a topic so central to making effective oral submissions that it is accorded the next chapter all to itself.

## Basics of speaking in court

10–2 Moot court advocacy is a form of public speaking. The subject matter of a moot may be more technical than a typical debate and the setting more stylised, but mooters, like all public speakers, must present arguments out loud in front of an audience. If they are to convey their arguments persuasively, mooters must accordingly acquire the skills needed for effective public speaking.

For some reason, the perception abounds that good public speakers are born, not made. Little could be farther from the truth. Almost anyone can learn how to speak in public effectively. You just need to work at it. If you require proof that public speaking can be taught, dip into the vast library of literature on the subject, starting with Aristotle's *Rhetoric* in about 360 BC.

The next few pages do not purport to add anything revolutionary to this body of work. They will instead focus briefly on six attributes that are fundamental to speaking effectively in moot courts: stance, demeanour, eye contact, vocal volume, pace of delivery and tone of delivery. You could write a book about each of them. Someone probably has.

### Stance

10–3 There are not too many ways in which mooting resembles golf, but stance is one of them. Just as you must address a golf ball using the correct stance, so you must adopt the right posture to address a moot judge. If you are slouched over your papers with your face directed at your feet, you will not only fail to project your voice, you will also give the judge the impression that you lack confidence in what you are saying. In such a position, there is little chance of sending your submissions safely down the middle of the mooting fairway.

There is nothing complicated about adopting a proper stance. Stick to the following guidelines and you will not go too far wrong:

- Stand straight or lean very slightly forward from the waist.

- Hold your head up, even if you are looking down.

- Push your shoulders back so that you do not appear hunched.

- Keep your hands down, whether they are in front of you, at your sides or behind your back. If you are holding your notes in front of you, your hands should ideally be somewhere between the level of your waistband and your chest.

- Keep your hands out of your pockets.

- If there is a lectern, by all means rest your hands on it. But the operative word is "rest". Avoid gripping both sides of the lectern or you will look as though you are at the wheel of a four-ton lorry.

## Demeanour

The manner in which you comport yourself as you speak is hugely important. If you sway  **10–4** from side-to-side or gesticulate excessively, for example, you will distract the judge from what you are saying and undermine your efforts to appear confident. If, on the other hand, every movement of your body is purposeful, you will appear poised and in control even if the judge has just asked you a question and you do not have the foggiest idea how to answer it.

You can project a favourable demeanour from the moment when you stand up to begin your oral submissions. Look the judge in the eyes and smile briefly. Then, as you deliver your submissions, consciously guard against fidgeting. If you are prone, for example, to clicking your pen on and off or twiddling it in your fingers as you speak, force yourself not to pick it up in the first place. If you have a tendency to gesture frequently with your hands, put them to work holding your notes.

## Eye contact

Look the judge in the eyes as often as you can and for as long as you can. You should be  **10–5** trying to engage him in a form of conversation. When you have conversations with friends, you do not direct your remarks to a point six inches above their heads or to floorboards beneath your feet. You look them in the eyes. Do the same with the judge. Hold his gaze and he will have no option but to concentrate on what you are saying.

Regular eye contact with the judge will also enable you to watch what he is doing. Is he paying attention to your masterful analysis of the moot problem or does he look lost? You need to know. If the judge appears not to be following a particular submission, you may have to repeat or rephrase it. Looking up frequently will also enable you to see when the judge is writing something down. If he is, follow his pen and wait for it to stop moving before you launch into your next point.

If your moot tribunal consists of more than one judge, make eye contact with each of them separately. You are, in effect, addressing a small audience and you need to make sure that every member of that audience is fully engaged with what you are saying.

## Vocal volume

**10–6** If judges are to follow your oral submissions, they have to hear them. You must therefore speak up. There is no need to deliver your submissions in a booming *basso-profondo*. Just make a conscious effort to speak at a higher volume than you ordinarily would in conversation and to project your voice from your lungs rather than from your throat.

And remember this: whilst judges frequently complain that the mooters who appear before them speak too softly, you will be almost unique in the annals of mooting history if the judge criticises you for speaking too loudly.

## Pace of delivery

**10–7** There is something about speaking in public that causes the brain to believe that the mouth is talking at about two-thirds of its actual speed. You believe that you are speaking at normal conversational pace when you sound to the outside world like a horse-racing commentator as the field enters the final furlong. For mooters, this cerebral deception can have unfortunate consequences. For one thing, speaking too quickly makes them sound nervous. More importantly, oral submissions delivered at breakneck pace lose much of their potency because judges struggle to follow them.

You should therefore remind yourself repeatedly to slow down. If it helps, write the words "slow down" at the top of every page of your notes. For just as it is almost impossible to speak too loudly, it is extremely difficult to speak too slowly.

Now and again, you should not be afraid to bring your delivery to a complete standstill. A short silence—and, be warned, the shortest silence will seem like an age to you—will quickly grab the judge's attention if you are worried that his mind is drifting from the point that you are making. Silence is also a useful way of adding emphasis if it follows immediately after a particularly important submission.

## Tone of delivery

**10–8** The judge will start to lose interest in your oral submissions if you deliver them in a flat monotone. You should therefore vary the pitch of your voice occasionally. The variations must sound natural, however. You should place emphasis only on words that merit it, just as you would when you speak casually with friends. Try, therefore, to avoid what linguists call "Australian questioning intonation", whereby the pitch of the voice rises at the end of each sentence to the level of a question even though no question is being asked. It is not natural. Unless, that is, you are Australian.

## Order and length of speeches

**10–9** The order in which mooters address the moot court is different in English law and Scots law moots. This divergence reflects the contrasting practices in the courts of the two jurisdictions. Figure 10.1 shows the usual order of speeches.

## Figure 10.1: Order of speeches

10–10

| Speech No. | England and Wales | Scotland |
|------------|-------------------|----------|
| 1. | Leading counsel for the appellant | Junior counsel for the appellant/reclaimer |
| 2. | Junior counsel for the appellant | Junior counsel for the respondent |
| 3. | Leading counsel for the respondent | Senior counsel for the appellant/reclaimer |
| 4. | Junior counsel for the respondent | Senior counsel for the respondent |
| 5. | Leading or junior counsel for the appellant (in reply) | N/A |

As appears from figure 10.1, in England and Wales, both teams speak one after the other with leading counsel speaking first and junior counsel following. Leading or junior counsel for the appellant then enjoys a right of reply at the end of the moot. In Scotland, by contrast, both sides' junior counsel speak before both sides' senior counsel, and it is the respondent that enjoys the last word.

In one important respect, however, the order of speeches is the same in both English and **10–11** Scots law moots: it is always the appellant's team that addresses the court first (albeit leading counsel in England and Wales, and junior counsel in Scotland). This arrangement reflects the fact that it is the appellant rather than the respondent who is coming to the moot court to seek a remedy.

The competition rules will stipulate how much speaking time each mooter is allowed. Typically it is in the order of 10 to 15 minutes. Leading or senior counsel are sometimes given more "air time" than junior counsel. In English law moots, reply submissions on behalf of the appellant are usually limited to no more than five minutes.

# Structure of oral submissions

Wherever you appear in the order of speeches, you must arrange your oral submissions **10–12** logically if you want to maximise their impact. No single arrangement will work for every moot speech. Nonetheless, it is possible to identify in broad terms the different segments of a typical speech and to suggest a logical order in which to organise them.

Once again, classical rhetoric is instructive. It recommends the following six-stage arrangement for a well-reasoned argument:

- introduction or *exordium*, in which the orator introduces the subject of the argument;

- background or *narratio*, in which the orator gives an account of the relevant factual history;

- division or *partitio*, in which the orator outlines the argument;

- proof or *confirmatio*, in which the orator provides logical reasons to support the argument;

- refutation or *refutatio*, in which the orator answers opposing points of view; and

- conclusion or *peroratio*, in which the orator sums up the argument.

Despite being more than two millennia old, this arrangement is remarkably relevant for mooting and will readily serve as a basic structure for your oral submissions. It will not always suit your purposes perfectly, however. In particular, the classical arrangement was designed for speeches in which an entire argument is advanced. In mooting, by contrast, a team's argument is presented over the course of two speeches. Moreover, as we shall see, it is only the first mooter to address the court who need offer the judge a summary of the facts. None of the subsequent mooters' speeches will therefore include the background stage of the classical arrangement.

**10–13**　　The meat of the classical arrangement lies in the proof and refutation stages. The amount of time that you devote to them in your oral submissions will depend to a large extent on where you appear in the order of speeches. In an English law moot, the appellant's counsel should use the vast majority of their opening speeches to develop their positive case. They will not have heard what the respondent's counsel have to say at that stage and should be wary of anticipating the detail of their arguments. The bulk of the appellant's refutation should accordingly be made in the reply submissions, after the respondent's counsel have spoken. Conversely, leading and junior counsel for the respondent will have heard the entirety of the appellant's positive case when they get to their feet. They should both therefore address the appellant's arguments during their speeches.

In Scots law moots, the dynamic is rather different because the mooters from each side speak alternately. Save for junior counsel for the appellant/reclaimer, who speaks first, each mooter therefore hears at least part of the other side's case before beginning his submissions. It is incumbent on all of the subsequent speakers to respond to what has gone before. The later that you appear in the speaking order, the more of the debate you will have heard and the more you will be expected to react to it in the course of your oral submissions.

The classical arrangement places the proof of the orator's argument before the refutation of any opposing arguments. As a general rule, this approach works well for moots. If possible, you should be aiming to define the debate in your own terms. It is usually easier to achieve that end if you lead off with your positive case before responding to what the other side has said. If you take the alternative approach and begin your submissions with a long list of attacks on your opponents' arguments, it might appear to the judge that you are simply reacting to the other side's case.

The next four sections of this chapter look at the content of oral submissions. They are organised broadly in line with the classical arrangement.

# Opening remarks

**10–14**　　The burden of making introductory remarks falls disproportionately on the first mooter to address the court. As appears from figure 10.1, the first speaker will be leading counsel for the appellant in an English law moot and junior counsel for the appellant/reclaimer in a Scots law moot. The manner in which the first speaker should open his or her oral submissions is considered next. There then follows a discussion about the introductory remarks of the subsequent speakers.

# First speaker

The first speaker's opening remarks should serve four principal purposes: to introduce the **10–15**
mooters from both teams; to explain the background to the moot; to outline the division of
labour between the appellant's counsel; and to ensure that the judge has received any
skeleton argument or bundle of authorities. Each of these objectives can be achieved using
relatively formulaic phraseology.

## *Introduction*

The introductions are easily accomplished. By way of example, in *Cecil v Dickens* the speech
of leading counsel for the appellant (since this is an English law moot problem) might begin
in the following way:

> "*May it please Your Lordship,*[1] *I am CJ Stryver and I appear on behalf of the appellant
> in this matter, Mr Charles Dickens, together with my learned friend Mr Carton. The
> respondent, Mr Henry Cecil, is represented by my learned friends Ms Mannering and Mr
> Thursby.*"

There are three short points to note about these introductory words:　　　　　　　**10–16**

- The phrase "*May it please your Lordship, . . .*" is a rather formal way to start a speech.
  Nonetheless, it is widely used, both by mooters and practitioners. A less grandiose
  option is to say simply, "*My Lord, . . .*".

- You do not need to mention your own name if it is clear that the judge already knows
  perfectly well who you are. Drop it, for example, if the judge calls on you by name to
  begin your oral submissions.

- As you introduce your fellow mooters to the judge, glance briefly towards each of
  them in turn. This gesture will help the judge to work out who is who.

## *Background*

Having effected the introductions, the first speaker should next explain what the moot is
about. This explanation effectively covers the first two stages of the classical arrangement.
You can provide it quite quickly. In *Cecil v Dickens*, for example, leading counsel for the
appellant might follow his introduction with the following words:

> "*This is the hearing of the appeal against a decision of Mr Justice Steerforth sitting in the
> Queen's Bench Division. The learned judge held that Mr Dickens gave negligent advice to Mr
> Cecil in relation to a potential claim by Mr Cecil against a firm of accountants called
> Wickfield's.*"

Given that the moot judge will almost certainly have read the moot problem in advance of **10–17**
the moot, a short statement of this nature should suffice by way of background. However,
there is a convention in many mooting competitions that the first speaker should formally

---

[1] You would, of course, substitute here the words "Your Ladyship", "Your Ladyships" or "Your Lordships"
depending on the make-up of your moot tribunal. The same point applies to all of the examples in this chapter
and Chapter 11.

offer the judge a summary of the facts of the moot problem. You can make this offer with the words, *"would Your Lordship like to be reminded of the facts of this case?"* If you ask this question and the judge's response is affirmative, keep your summary of the facts short and do not proceed to read out large chunks of the moot problem verbatim. Focus instead on the broad subject matter of the claim and the stage that the proceedings have reached. In *Cecil v Dickens*, for instance, the appellant's leading counsel might summarise the facts in the following way:

> *"In these proceedings, Mr Cecil alleges that Mr Dickens, who is a practising solicitor, provided negligent advice to him in early 2002 about a potential claim against a firm of accountants called Wickfield's. The basis of Mr Cecil's claim is that Mr Dickens failed to mention that a limitation period applied to the potential action. The limitation period expired before Mr Cecil commenced proceedings. At the trial of this action in the Queen's Bench Division, Mr Justice Steerforth found Mr Dickens liable in negligence and ordered him to pay Mr Cecil the sum of £100,000. That sum represented the value that the judge ascribed to Mr Cecil's potential claim against Wickfield's."*

## Outline division of labour

The next task of the first speaker at a moot, which equates to the third stage of the classical arrangement, is to tell the judge in outline how the appellant's team intends to divide its oral submissions. More often than not, each member of a moot team will deal with a different ground of appeal. Thus, for example, the appellant's leading counsel in *Cecil v Dickens* might set the agenda for his team's submissions in the following way:

> *"As Your Lordship will see from the moot problem, Mr Dickens relies on two grounds of appeal. The first is that he owed no duty of care in negligence to Mr Cecil. The second is that, even if he did owe a duty of care, he did not breach it. I will deal with the first ground of appeal in my speech. My learned junior will address Your Lordship on the second ground of appeal."*

## Skeletons and bundles

**10–18**  If the teams have prepared skeleton arguments and/or bundles of the authorities on which they rely, the first speaker's final task in opening is to ensure that the judge has received the documents that the appellant's team has served. You might be able to see that the judge has your skeleton and bundle in front of him. But if you are not sure, you might ask as follows:

> *"My Lord, before I move on to the first of my submissions, can I confirm that Your Lordship has received copies of the appellant's skeleton argument and bundle of authorities?"*

If, by some misfortune, the judge answers "no" to this question, you will be able to hand up the spare copies of your team's skeleton argument and bundle that you brought to the moot in dutiful observance of the advice contained in Chapter 8.

## Illustration

For ease of reference, figure 10.2 draws together the various elements of the first speaker's opening remarks described above. It assumes that the first speaker does not formally offer the judge a summary of the facts of the moot problem.

## Figure 10.2: Opening remarks of the first speaker

**10–19**

> May it please Your Lordship, I am CJ Stryver and I appear on behalf of the appellant in this matter, Mr Charles Dickens, together with my learned friend Mr Carton. The respondent, Mr Henry Cecil, is represented by my learned friends Ms Mannering and Mr Thursby.
>
> This is the hearing of the appeal against a decision of Mr Justice Steerforth sitting in the Queen's Bench Division. The learned judge held that Mr Dickens gave negligent advice to Mr Cecil in relation to a potential claim by Mr Cecil against a firm of accountants called Wickfield's.
>
> As Your Lordship will see from the moot problem, Mr Dickens relies on two grounds of appeal. The first is that he owed no duty of care in negligence to Mr Cecil. The second is that, even if he did owe a duty of care, he did not breach it. I will deal with the first ground of appeal in my speech. My learned junior will address Your Lordship on the second ground of appeal.
>
> My Lord, before I move on to the first of my submissions, can I confirm that Your Lordship has received copies of the appellant's skeleton argument and bundle of authorities?

# Subsequent speakers

In comparison with the first speaker, the subsequent speakers have relatively little to say by **10–20** way of opening remarks. In particular, there is no need for them to provide another summary of the factual background. What each of them will say depends to a large extent on where they appear in the speaking order.

*First speaker for the respondent*

As appears from figure 10.1, in an English law moot, the first member of the respondent's team to speak is leading counsel, who appears third in the order of speeches. In Scots law moots, the first speaker for the respondent is junior counsel, who appears second.

The opening remarks of this mooter should introduce the respondent's team and provide a short agenda for the respondent's submissions. In all likelihood, that agenda will mirror the division of labour between the appellant's counsel. For example, leading counsel for the respondent in *Cecil v Dickens* might begin her submissions in the following way:

> *"May it please Your Lordship, my name is Sally Mannering. Together with my learned junior, Mr Thursby, I represent the respondent, Mr Cecil. My learned junior and I have divided our submissions in the same way as my learned friends opposite. I will therefore address Your Lordship on the first ground of appeal, namely whether a duty of care arises in negligence. My learned junior will then deal with the second ground of appeal— whether there has been a breach of duty."*

If the parties have prepared skeleton arguments and/or bundles of authorities, the first speaker for the respondent should also check that the judge has received copies of the documents that the respondent's team has served.

*Second speakers for both teams*

In an English law moot, junior counsel for both teams follow leading counsel. In Scots law moots, the order is reversed. The opening remarks of the second speaker in each team should set the agenda for their own submissions, ideally by reference to the arguments already advanced by their team-mates. In *Cecil v Dickens*, for example, junior counsel for the appellant might open his submissions in this way:

> "*May it please Your Lordship, I am Sydney Carton, junior counsel for Mr Dickens. My learned leader has already addressed Your Lordship on Mr Dickens's first ground of appeal. I will now address Your Lordship on the second ground of appeal. My submissions will therefore address whether Mr Dickens breached any duty of care that he is found to have owed to Mr Cecil.*"

### Appellant in reply (English law moots only)

Depending on the competition rules, the reply submissions may be made by leading or junior counsel for the appellant. Whoever undertakes the task can keep their opening remarks to a minimum. You might even say as little as this: "*May it please Your Lordship, I have* [three] *points in reply.*"

## Developing your positive case

**10–21** With the opening remarks safely negotiated, you can proceed to develop your team's positive case on the ground or grounds of appeal allocated to you. The arguments that you present at this stage will be those that you constructed and honed when you researched the law and that are summarised in any skeleton that your team served in advance of the moot. However, you will be able to descend into far greater detail during your oral submissions than you could in your skeleton argument.

## The building blocks

As you articulate your team's positive case, you must convey to the judge the logical reasoning that underpins your arguments. As Chapter 3 explained, most of the arguments that you make at a moot will be founded on deductive reasoning and will have three strands: a major premise, a minor premise and a conclusion. These strands translate into the following steps when you develop an argument orally:

**Major premise**  Identify the precise proposition of law on which you rely and take the judge through the authority that you contend supports that proposition.

**Minor premise**  Apply the proposition of law to the facts of the moot problem by highlighting those facts that you assert are relevant.

**Conclusion**  Explain the outcome that you argue follows from the application of the proposition of law to the facts.

# Referring to authorities

The bulk of your oral submissions is likely to be spent walking the judge through the authorities on which you rely. Whenever you take the judge to one of your authorities, it is vitally important that he understands what you are showing him and why. If the judge does not appreciate the principle that you are drawing from your authority, your argument will be significantly undermined.

**10–22** You should be able to avoid this pitfall by following the seven steps outlined below when you take the judge to a new authority during your oral submissions. It is heavily skewed towards case reports because these are the authorities that mooters most often refer to inadequately. There are, of course, other ways of achieving the same ends. As you gain in experience, you will discover what works best for you.

## Step 1: explain the relevance of the authority

Before you ask the judge to read an authority, you must explain why you contend that it is relevant. Without an introduction of this nature, the judge will not understand what you want him to glean from the authority when he reads it. If, for example, you refer to an authority that you assert contains a summary of the relevant legal principles, you might introduce it as follows: "*My Lord, in my submission, the relevant principles of law were recently explained in the case of . . .* ".

## Step 2: cite the authority

If neither team has previously referred to the authority during the moot, you must next cite it correctly. The written and oral forms of case and other citations are slightly different. You cannot therefore simply read out the written version. Table 10.3 includes three examples of the written and oral versions of the same citations. Note, in particular, that in case report citations the letter "v" is always pronounced "and" or "against" rather than "vee" or "versus", and that the letter "R" is always pronounced "the Crown" rather than "are".

## Table 10.3: Written and oral forms of citations of authority

**10–23**

| Written citation | Oral citation |
|---|---|
| *Commissioners of Customs and Excise v Barclays Bank plc* [2006] 3 WLR 1 | "Commissioners of Customs and Excise against Barclays Bank plc, which is reported in volume three of the *Weekly Law Reports* for 2006 at page one." |
| *R v Jackson* [1999] 1 All ER 572 | "The Crown against Jackson, reported in the first volume of the *All England Law Reports* for 1999 at page 572." |
| *Jackson & Powell on Professional Negligence*, 5th ed (2002) | "Jackson and Powell on Professional Negligence, fifth edition, which was published in 2002." |

## Step 3: ensure that the judge has a copy of the authority

Once you have cited the authority, you should make sure that the judge has a copy of it. If you are providing your authorities to the judge one by one, this is the point at which you should hand up a copy of the authority (via the moot court clerk if there is one). If you have served a bundle of authorities in advance of the moot, you should identify the tab or page number at which the authority appears.

### Step 4: if the authority is a reported case, offer the judge a summary of the facts

When you refer to a reported decision that has not previously been cited at the moot, you should offer to provide the judge with a summary of the facts. You might do this by asking, *"is Your Lordship familiar with the facts of this case?"* or *"would Your Lordship like to be reminded of the facts of this case?"* The judge will often be well aware of the case and will decline your offer. There will be occasions, however, when the judge is not familiar with the decision and indicates that a reminder of the salient facts would assist. You should then provide your summary.[2]

### Step 5: identify the relevant passage of the authority

You should now identify the passage of the authority that you want the judge to read. You must do so carefully and slowly. Many a mooter has left a judge floundering by trotting out a page number and then launching immediately into a quotation. There are various ways of identifying the relevant passage. For example, you might say, *"may I refer Your Lordship to the judgment of Lord [ ] at paragraph [ ] of the report?"* or, *"would Your Lordship please turn to page [ ] of the report? The relevant passage starts about two-thirds of the way down the page with the words [ ]."*

Having told the judge precisely where the relevant passage is located, you must make sure that he has found it before you take the next step. If you see that the judge is still flicking through the case report, give him a moment or two to find the right place. If he is staring around blankly, repeat the reference.

### Step 6: read the relevant passage of the authority

You should read the passage on which you rely when, and only when, you are satisfied that the judge is actually looking at it. If the passage is no more than about seven or eight lines long, you should read it out loud unless the judge tells you not to. You can then place emphasis on the words that you regard as important. If the passage is any longer, you should first ask the judge whether he would like you to read it. He may tell you that he would rather read it to himself, in which case you should remain silent until it is clear that he has finished.

### Step 7: apply the authority to the facts

Once the judge has seen the passage of the authority on which you rely, you must explain how it applies to the facts of the moot problem. If the passage is quite lengthy, it may assist the judge if you first distill it into a more pithy legal principle.

## Illustration

This section would not be complete without an illustration. Figure 10.4 therefore contains an example oral submission based on the possible line of argument identified in figure 3.3 in

---

[2] As explained in Chapter 5, the notes that you prepare for the moot should include summaries of the facts of each of the reported cases on which you rely. You can then refer to these notes at this point in your oral submissions.

Chapter 3. The submission is made on behalf of the appellant in relation to the first ground of appeal in *Cecil v Dickens*. It includes each of the seven steps outlined above. In the interests of manageability, figure 10.4 is an abbreviated version of what you might actually say in practice and includes a number of explanatory notes in bold.

## Figure 10.4: Oral submission referring to authority

> With Your Lordship's permission, I now turn to consider whether Mr Dickens owed a duty of care to Mr Cecil in negligence to avoid pure economic loss. In my submission, the proper approach for determining this issue is the so-called "multi-test" approach. This test was recently applied by the House of Lords in Commissioners of Customs and Excise against Barclays Bank plc. The case is reported in volume three of the *Weekly Law Reports* for 2006 at page one.
> **At this point, you would hand up a copy of the authority to the judge or identify the relevant tab or page number of your bundle of authorities**.
> Is Your Lordship familiar with the facts of this case?
> **If the judge answered "no", you would provide a summary**.
> Would Your Lordship please turn to paragraph 82 of the report, which is part of the judgment of Lord Mance?
> **You would then wait until you were certain that the judge had found this passage**.
> The passage on which I rely starts at the first sentence of the paragraph. It reads as follows:
>
> *"The conceptual basis on which courts decide whether a duty of care exists in particular circumstances has been repeatedly examined. Three broad approaches have been suggested, involving consideration of (a) whether there has been an assumption of responsibility, (b) whether a three-fold test of foreseeability, proximity and "fairness, justice and reasonableness" has been satisfied or (c) whether the alleged duty would be "incremental" to previous cases."*
>
> Lord Mance then proceeded to apply each of these tests in turn.
> **You might next take the judge to each passage in the judgment in which Lord Mance applied these tests**.
> In my submission, none of the three approaches identified by Lord Mance is satisfied in this case. The first test is whether there has been an assumption of responsibility. Would Your Lordship please now look at the moot problem?
> **You would wait until you were certain that the judge had the moot problem in front of him**.
> Your Lordship will see that, during the contentious conversation between the parties in January 2002, Mr Dickens told Mr Cecil that, *"If you decide to take matters forward, you should consult a law firm called Barkis & Traddles, which specialises in litigation."* In my submission, these words would have made it quite clear to Mr Cecil that Mr Dickens was not assuming responsibility towards him. On the contrary, Mr Dickens was explicitly telling Mr Cecil that he should consult another solicitor if he wanted to proceed with his claim against Wickfield's. In those circumstances, it is submitted that Mr Cecil cannot possibly satisfy the first limb of the multi-test approach.
> **You would then proceed to make submissions on each of the remaining tests identified by Lord Mance**.

**10–24**

# Refuting your opponents' arguments

The penultimate stage of the classical arrangement for a well reasoned argument is refutation. In mooting terms, refutation is that part of the oral submissions when you attempt to knock some of the stuffing out of your opponents' arguments. The submissions

**10–25**

that you make by way of refutation will depend entirely on the arguments that your opponents present. Each of your attacks should go to the substance of the other side's case. You will gain little, for example, by nit picking over relatively trivial matters such as incorrect citations of authority. The sorts of points that you should be looking for are discussed in Chapter 3 and are not repeated here. You ought to be able to identify a number of them in advance of the moot, particularly if your opponents serve a skeleton argument. You are likely to find, however, that other ideas occur to you at the moot itself, especially when your opponents are on their feet.

The most straightforward way of presenting your arguments in refutation is to deal with them all in a group at the end of your speech. If you take this course, you should indicate to the judge after you have finished developing your positive case that you are about to address a selection of the other side's points. You might do so by saying, for example, *"My learned friends opposite made* [three] *points that I would like to address briefly before concluding my submissions."* You would then go through these points one by one, preferably in the same order as your opponents advanced them.

An alternative approach is to make each of your criticisms of the other side's case immediately after making the corresponding point of your positive case. Say, for example, that your opponents have cited a reported case in which the decision differed from a case on which you rely. Having taken the judge to your authority and explained why it applies to the facts of the moot problem, you might address your opponents' authority as follows:

> *"My learned friend opposite relied on the case of* [name of case] *as authority for the proposition that* [summarise the proposition]. *In my submission, this decision is of no assistance to Your Lordship for* [three] *reasons. First, . . . Second, . . . Third, . . ."*

**10–26**     This discussion has assumed that you follow the classical arrangement and make your arguments in refutation collectively or individually after the arguments that comprise your positive case. You should not regard this arrangement as inflexible, however. In fact, there are occasions when it can be extremely effective to *precede* your positive case with a point of refutation. This approach works best if it is confined to a single point on an important issue that you can deliver swiftly. If you find yourself in this position, you might launch your attack in this way: *"My Lord, before I turn to my first submission, I would like briefly to pick up on a point that my learned friends opposite have relied on. . . ."* What you must then avoid is becoming bogged down in the detail of your opponents' argument. This approach requires a commando raid of a submission. You need to go in quickly, score your point and then return to base.

## Concluding remarks

**10–27**     Compared to advocates in professional practice, the amount of speaking time at the disposal of mooters is very short. Mooters are not therefore expected to conclude their oral submissions with a comprehensive summary of what they said only a few minutes previously. It is nonetheless worth rounding off your speech with a few well-turned, up-beat sentences. You must also explain to the judge exactly what remedy your team is seeking.

You might begin your closing remarks with the words, *"In conclusion, . . ."* or *"To conclude, . . ."*. Alternatively, you can simply pause after you finish your final substantive submission and start your conclusion with the words, *"My Lord, . . ."*.

You should always end your oral submissions with the words, *"Unless I can be of any further assistance to Your Lordship, those are my submissions/that concludes my submissions."* This formula, which is used in practice as well as mooting, lets the judge know that you have reached the end of your speech and gives him a chance to ask any final questions. Nine times out of ten, the judge will not take up the invitation and you will be able to sit down.

Figure 10.5 contains an example of how junior counsel for the appellant (i.e. the second speaker) in the illustrative case of *Cecil v Dickens* might round off his oral submissions.

## Figure 10.5: Concluding remarks

10–28

> My Lord, as my learned friend Mr Stryver explained during his speech, this case does not satisfy the test that the English courts have most recently applied in order to determine whether a duty of care arises in negligence to avoid pure economic loss. In any event, even if Your Lordship were to find that Mr Dickens did owe a duty of care to Mr Cecil, Mr Dickens did not breach that duty for the reasons that I have outlined in my speech. It is therefore submitted that this appeal should be allowed. Unless I can be of any further assistance to Your Lordship, those are my submissions.

# Tips for making oral submissions

The last four sections of this chapter have looked at the different parts of a typical moot  10–29
speech. The next few pages, by contrast, contain a number of hints and suggestions that apply throughout your oral submissions.

## Provide regular "signposts"

Throughout your oral submissions, you should give the judge periodic indications of  10–30
where your argument is heading. Without these "signposts", your submissions will be difficult to follow. A short selection of "signposts" is described below:

- **Lists**
  One of the most effective ways of keeping the judge clear about the direction and structure of your submissions is to make regular use of lists: explain that you have a certain number of points to make on a particular issue and then go through them one by one. For example, towards the beginning of your speech, you might say this: *"My Lord, in support of the first ground of appeal, I have three submissions. They are, first, that . . . , second, that . . . and, third, that . . . . Turning to my first submission, . . ."*.

- **Connecting phrases**
  You will often want to make connections between your various points and must ensure that the judge understands the links that you are attempting to establish. You might, for instance, identify a proposition of law and then refer the judge to an authority from which you contend that it derives. Having stated the proposition, you might say, *"In support of this submission, I rely on the case of . . ."*, or *"In my submission, this principle was applied in the case of . . ."*. Other, shorter, connecting phrases include "as a result", *"for example"*, and "in summary".

- **Separating phrases**
  Just as important as linking your submissions together is distinguishing between the different points that you make during your speech. There are various ways of signalling to the judge that you are moving from one point to the next. They include, for instance, *"My Lord, I now turn to consider . . ."*, *"My Lord, my next point/ submission is . . ."*, and *"In conclusion, . . ."*.

Do not be afraid of appearing overly simplistic when you make use of "signposts". The judge will not be as familiar as you are with the material and will probably be delighted to receive a "steer".

## Highlight the judge's helpful interventions

10–31    Not unnaturally, judges tend to be rather fond of the points that they think of themselves. If the judge makes an observation that is helpful to your case, whether during your oral submissions or someone else's, try to weave a reference to it into your speech. You might do so, for example, by saying the following: *"As Your Lordship rightly pointed out to my learned friend Ms Mannering, . . ."*; or, *"In my submission, this is no more than a natural extension of the point that Your Lordship made to me a moment ago."*

## Use your skeleton argument effectively

10–32    If you have served a skeleton argument in advance of the moot, you should put it to good use during your oral submissions. The judge will have read it and will expect you to develop the arguments contained in it during your speech. If you fail to tie your oral submissions back to your skeleton, you risk confusing the judge about what your case really is.

There are two easy ways of achieving this linkage. The first is to present your arguments in the same order as they appear in your skeleton. The logic inherent in your skeleton should then be preserved in your oral submissions.[3] The second is to refer directly to your skeleton from time to time during your speech. You might, for example, say this: *"As Your Lordship will have seen from paragraph [ ] of the appellant's skeleton argument, the appellant relies in support of this submission on the case of . . ."*.

The references that you make to your team's skeleton should be brief. In particular, you should not read out large chunks of your skeleton argument word-for-word.

## Avoid the following:

10–33    Some things do not work well in moot speeches and you should avoid them. What follows is a short list of some of the most common offenders:

- **Jokes**
  Whilst the occasional amusing comment can go down very well, particularly if it comes to you on the spur of the moment, prepared "gags" almost always founder.

---

[3] Chapter 4 discusses the logical order for submissions in skeleton arguments.

However funny you might think them when you prepare your oral submissions, they are likely to induce pin-drop silence or embarrassed titters when you deliver them.

● **Analogies**
Analogies very rarely work. For the most part, they are either so different from or so similar to the facts that the mooter compares them with that they add nothing meaningful to the argument.

● **Bashing brick walls**
If you have made a submission as persuasively as you can and the judge has indicated that he is not convinced by it, do not proceed to repeat it using slightly different language in the hope that he will change his mind. Move on to your next point.

● **Literary quotes**
Desist from making extensive quotes from classic literature. A Hamlet soliloquy carries no persuasive force in a moot court (except, perhaps, to persuade the judge that you have completely lost your marbles).

● *Ad hominem* **attacks**
Do not make personal comments about your opponents even if they make snide comments about you or your team-mate.

# Time management

As explained earlier in this chapter, mooting competition rules invariably impose time **10–34** restrictions on each speaker's oral submissions. You should ensure that you observe them. Many mooters get into difficulties with timing. Some are overly ambitious about how much they can say in the time available, then panic when they discover that their time is up and garble what remains of their submissions. Other mooters, conversely, underestimate how quickly they will complete their submissions and are forced to sit down with valuable speaking time unutilised.

The first step in managing your time properly is knowing in advance of the moot how long your prepared submissions should last. Timing your submissions should therefore be part of every mooter's practice regimen.[4] But you can never know when you are practising your submissions precisely how long they will take at the moot, particularly if your allotted time includes interventions from the bench. You therefore need to build flexibility into your oral submissions.

In order to avoid running drastically over your allotted time, prepare in advance a **10–35** conclusion of a specific length. In most moots, you will receive some warning (usually from the moot court clerk) as you approach the end of your allotted speaking time. If you know that you will be given a 30-second warning, for example, you should prepare a conclusion that lasts for this amount of time.[5] Wherever you are in your speech when you receive your warning, you can then complete the point that you are making and skip quickly to the start of your conclusion. If you are not going to receive a warning, you can prepare a shorter

---

[4] Chapter 7 considers in detail how to practise oral submissions.
[5] By way of example, the remarks in figure 10.5 should take approximately 30 seconds to deliver.

conclusion of perhaps 15 seconds. If your time expires before you complete your submissions, you can then jump to it in the knowledge that you will exceed your allotted time only marginally.

You can plan for the eventuality of finishing more quickly than you anticipated by having an additional prepared submission up your sleeve. It would not, of course, be one of your central points; those you will make first. But you would be able to resort to it if you found that you had more time at the end of your speech than you thought you would.

# Non-speaking mooters

**10–36** You can have a significant impact on the course of the oral submissions even when you are seated. A display of bad manners can certainly damage your prospects of success, as Chapter 9 explains. But non-speaking mooters can make a positive contribution too. Their role differs somewhat according to whether the speaker is the mooter's team-mate or an opponent.

## Team-mate speaking

**10–37** When your team-mate is speaking, your principal task is to provide whatever help you can without drawing attention to yourself. The assistance that you render might include any of the following:

- **Helping with judicial interventions**
  You can probably be of most assistance if your partner is struggling to answer one of the judge's questions. If you have thought of a satisfactory response, you should communicate it to your team-mate either by scribbling something down on a piece of paper or a "post-it" note or, if the judge gives permission, by consulting your partner quickly and quietly. What you should never do is attempt to address the judge directly.

- **Helping with references to documents**
  If your team-mate has given the judge an incorrect page reference to an authority or is unable to recall a reference with sufficient speed, you should be poised with the correct information.

- **Helping with practicalities**
  Your team-mate might need practical assistance for a number of reasons. He may have mislaid his pen and needs to jot something down. You can pass him yours. Alternatively, you may have noticed that his gown is sliding inexorably down his back. You might then pass him a note to warn of the impending disappearance of the offending garment.

- **Helping with pace**
  If your team-mate is talking too quickly, signal to him to slow down, perhaps with an inconspicuous hand gesture. Likewise, if he is spending too long on a particular topic, usher him on to the next point.

It goes without saying that, in order to provide assistance of this type, you have to follow with some care both your team-mate's submissions and the documents to which he is referring. Ideally, you should be one step ahead of your team-mate so that, if he trips up in some way, you are ready to intervene.

## Opponent speaking

Your primary objective when an opponent is making oral submissions is to get a decent note **10–38** of any points to which you or your partner should respond during your speeches. If you have prepared thoroughly for the moot, you should already have a pretty good idea of what the other side is going to say. But your opponents will inevitably make submissions during their speeches that you have not pre-empted.

Drafting effective notes when one of your opponents is speaking is a difficult skill to master. Your notes must be sufficiently detailed to convey the gist of the point being made and must also provide an adequate prompt for you to make your submission in reply. Yet, as you write your note, you cannot lose track of what your opponent is saying.

You will, of course, develop your own methodology of note-taking. Nonetheless, the following tips might help:

- **Keep your note short**
  You will not have much time in which to write your note and even less in which to read it when you refute the point during your speech. So try to keep your note brief.

- **Make a note of your opponent's actual words**
  When you note down the gist of an opponent's submission, it usually helps to record the key words or phrases that he actually used. You are far more likely to summarise a submission accurately during your speech, and the judge is more likely to recall it, if you have a few verbatim quotes in front of you.

- **Separate your opponent's submission from your response**
  Your notes will be more readily comprehensible if you clearly delineate what your opponent said from the point that you intend to make by way of refutation. At a minimum, these two elements of your note should begin on separate lines. You might even consider using differently coloured pens.

## Summary

The paramount skill that mooters must develop is an ability to present oral arguments **10–39** persuasively. This chapter has endeavoured to sketch out the fundamentals of what is a complicated skill. It has, in particular:

- Identified the six principal attributes required to speak effectively in a moot court.

- Explained the order in which mooters speak.

- Described how to structure a moot speech.
- Discussed the contents of each of the principal parts of a moot speech.
- Provided a number of tips for making oral submissions.
- Outlined the role of non-speaking mooters.

# 11 Judicial interventions

Unless you appear before an unusually docile moot judge, your oral submissions will be **11–1** punctuated by one or more interventions from the bench. Many mooters contemplate the prospect of judicial interventions with morbid dread. The purpose of this chapter is to shed some light on this murky subject and, in the process, to dispel some of the fear associated with it. The chapter begins with a quick look at what judicial interventions are, before considering the key to answering them effectively: thorough preparation. It then provides a number of practical suggestions for dealing with judicial interventions and runs through a list of sample questions. The chapter concludes by discussing how to cope with the most feared beast of the mooting deep: the question to which you don't know the answer.

## What is a judicial intervention?

A judicial intervention is a question asked by the moot judge. You should expect the judge **11–2** to interrupt you with questions several times during your oral submissions. He may also ask you one or more questions after you have completed your prepared submissions, but before you sit down. Most moot judges will try to ensure that they subject both sides to a similar level of questioning.

The power of judges to ask questions is an important feature of mooting. It enables them to test mooters' familiarity with the material, their ability to think on their feet and their overall skills as advocates. As a result, the manner in which mooters respond to judicial interventions often plays a central part in determining who wins a moot. Indeed, the winning team is sometimes the one that gives the more cogent and articulate responses to the judge's questions, even if its prepared submissions are the less impressive.

Judicial interventions therefore present you with a real opportunity to influence the judge. You should welcome them. Indeed, as your experience as a mooter grows, you are likely to find that the moots in which you perform at your best are those in which the judge asks the most penetrating questions.

## Preparation, preparation, preparation

The key to dealing effectively with judicial interventions is preparation. If you have prepared **11–3** properly for the moot, you will be able to cope with just about anything that the judge can conceivably throw at you. If the judge requests information or clarification, for example, the relevant knowledge should be at your fingertips. If the judge makes a pertinent criticism of one of your arguments, you should be able to fashion a suitable riposte. If the judge's question is irrelevant, you should be able to recognise it as such and deal with it accordingly.

The critical role of preparation in answering questions from the bench doubtless explains why advanced advocacy texts tend not to discuss judicial interventions as a distinct topic. They evidently assume that the advocate with full command of his brief will be able to deal effectively with any sensible question that the judge might ask. While this assumption is undoubtedly correct, there are nonetheless certain ways in which you can target your preparation so as to be ready for the judge's interventions.

# Targeting your preparation

11–4    Set out below are several steps that you can take to identify the key issues on which the judge is likely to concentrate his questions. By identifying these issues, you will be able to focus your preparation for judicial interventions more accurately. The goal here is not to work out *precisely* what the judge will ask (that would be impossible without the aid of a crystal ball). It is rather to anticipate the information or arguments that you will need to have readily to hand when the judge intervenes.

### *Identify the weaknesses in your case*

Given that moot problems are specifically designed to provide strengths and weaknesses to both sides, your arguments will inevitably have a soft underbelly. This vulnerable area is where the judge is most likely to target his questions. As part of your preparation for the moot, you should therefore identify all of the weak points in your arguments and consider how you can defend them from the sorts of questions that the judge might ask.

### *Look carefully at your opponents' authorities and skeleton argument*

A careful review of the materials served by the other side can give you all sorts of clues to the questions that may come up. Focus on the fundamental differences between your arguments and your opponents'. Look out, for example, for any authorities cited by your opponents that appear to be at odds with authorities on which your team is relying. If you find any, you can anticipate that the judge may well ask you why he should prefer your authority to that cited by your opponents.

### *Prepare with your team-mate*

It is always a good idea to practise your submissions out loud in front of your team-mate at least once before the moot.[1] Your team-mate should play the role of the judge and intervene frequently. You can then practise handling interruptions. Your partner may even alight on some of the very questions that the judge asks. Once you and your partner have both run through your speeches, you can deliberate together about any interventions that caused particular problems. If you cannot manage to hold a practice session like this, at least make

---

[1] Chapter 7 discusses why and how to practise oral submissions.

sure that you have a general brainstorming session with your mooting partner to discuss what the judge might ask each of you.

*Assume that the judge will ask sensible questions*

Your preparation for judicial interventions need only extend to those issues that the judge's questions might *reasonably* cover. Students who fear the judge asking them *anything* are causing themselves unnecessary worry. After all, an irrelevant, far-out question can be dealt with as such.

# Having the information at your fingertips

Once you have identified the issues that the judge is likely to focus on during his judicial **11–5** interventions, you must ensure that you are ready to deal with his questions. In particular, you should have readily available the information that you need to answer them. In the first place, this requires you to achieve a certain familiarity with the relevant material, that is to say the issues raised by the moot problem, the information that you have amassed in the course of your legal research and the arguments that you have developed. If you are *conversant* with this material—literally, able to talk about it without notes—you have a good chance of being able to recall it when you are on your feet at the moot. This proficiency should come from working with the material in the build-up to the moot.

It is, however, a rare person indeed who has all of the information required to get through a moot on the tip of his or her tongue. You should therefore prepare well organised, user-friendly notes to help you to find the specifics when you need them quickly. If, for example, you have identified a number of questions that the judge might ask during your oral submissions, make sure that your notes for the moot include brief answers to each of them.[2]

# Tips for answering judicial questions

Your preparation for the moot may have been sufficiently thorough to provide you with the **11–6** information that you need to answer a particular question from the judge, but it is still possible to deal with it ineffectively. If you jump in and attempt to answer it too quickly, for example, you might miss something that the judge said and provide only a partial response. The other potential pitfalls are too numerous to mention. You should be able to avoid them, however, by following these guidelines:

- **Listen carefully to the question**
  This is Rule Number One. If you do not listen to the question, you will not know what it is. If you do not know what it is, you cannot answer it properly. Listening carefully to the question means listening to all of it. Let the judge finish speaking before you commence your response.[3]

---

[2] Chapter 5 discusses in detail how to prepare notes for moots.
[3] As discussed in Chapter 9, interrupting the judge is not only dangerous, it is also a breach of mooting etiquette.

- **Make sure that you understand the question**

  In the heat of the moment, you may not follow precisely what the judge says. Do not be embarrassed to ask him to repeat the question. On the contrary, it is imperative that you do so. You might simply say as follows: *"Would Your Lordship please repeat/ rephrase the question?"* Another, slightly lengthier, option is to say, *"I am afraid that I did not entirely follow Your Lordship's question. Would Your Lordship please repeat it?"* If you are still not clear what the judge is asking, reformulate his question and ask him to confirm that your understanding is correct.

- **Take a moment before speaking**

  Unless the judge's question gives of a short and straightforward answer, it is usually sensible to wait for a moment or two after he has finished speaking before you launch into your response. Even if you already have a good idea of what you want to say, the extra time will help you to compose your answer. It will also allow you to consider whether your intended response might prejudice any of your team's arguments.

- **Give the judge a response there and then**

  Always provide an answer to the judge's question when he asks it. Mooters often reply to judicial interventions by saying, *"I will deal with Your Lordship's question later in my submissions."* This is a mistake. You should address the point straight away, if only briefly. You may be intending to deal with the issue later in your submissions, but that should not stop you from giving an immediate response, even if you preface it by saying, *"My Lord, I am intending to address this point in detail later in my submissions. In short, the answer is . . .".* If it makes sense to do so, you can even bring forward the submission that you were going to make and incorporate it into your reply. You will then demonstrate impressive flexibility and a command of the subject matter.

- **Watch out for the waffle**

  Do not turn into a waffle machine. It is horribly easy to drift into verbosity when the judge draws you away from your prepared material. Answer his question as succinctly and directly as you can. If you feel that your answer is wandering from the point, bring it swiftly to a close.

- **Never forget the basics of speaking in court**

  Some mooters let their guards down when they enter the "broken play" of responding to judicial interventions. Make sure that you continue to concentrate on the basics of courtroom advocacy: do not speak too quickly; do not start waving your arms around; and keep your eyes on the judge. You may even find, as many of the best mooters do, that your advocacy becomes less forced, more fluid and consequently more persuasive, when you respond to judicial interventions.

## Sample questions

**11–7** Some questions come up regularly at moots, whatever the subject matter of the moot problem. A selection of these "stock" questions is described below, together with some suggestions for how to answer them.

- *"I'm sorry. I didn't hear what you said."*or *"Can you please repeat your last point?"*
  Do not let these sorts of intervention throw you. The chances are that your voice did not carry to the bench or the judge may simply have "tuned out" for a moment or two when you were speaking. There is no need to craft an elaborate, clever answer to this type of question. Just repeat what you said. And stay cool. Nerves can make you babble even when faced with the simplest inquiry.

- *"What is the proposition that you derive from this authority?"*
  Whenever you refer the judge to an authority, you should clearly identify the legal principle that you derive from it.[4] If you are not explicit, this question is frequently the result. You ought to know off the top of your head why you are relying on each of your authorities, so should be able to tell the judge without difficulty.

- *"What persuasive force should I attribute to this authority?"* or *" Does this authority bind me?"*
  Many judges will ask one or other of these questions as a matter of course when you cite an authority from a foreign jurisdiction. The judge might also ask you this question if you rely on a decision of a court that is higher or lower than the moot court in the judicial hierarchy. If you are to answer these questions effectively, you must be familiar with the doctrine of *stare decisis* and how it applies.

- *"Why should I prefer your authority to your opponents'?"*
  An authority that you have cited may appear to conflict with an authority cited by your opponents. The judge may then want to know why he should accept yours. In response, you should explain to the judge why your opponents' authority can be distinguished from the moot problem. Your notes should include a list of the main distinguishing factors.

- *"Can you tell me whether this case has been considered in any subsequent decision?"*
  In order to elicit this type of question, you may have referred the judge to a helpful passage from a case reported some years ago. The judge, not unnaturally, wants to be satisfied that the passage still accurately reflects the law. This is essentially a straightforward factual question, to which you should have the answer if your research was adequate.

- *"If I understand you correctly, your submission is that . . . Is that right?"*
  If a judge says this to you, the chances are that he is struggling to understand a point that you are making or to see where it is going. Listen carefully to his reformulation of your submission. Do not agree with it unless you are quite confident that it is accurate. If the judge has missed something, do not be afraid to enlighten him.

- *"What do you say should happen in circumstances such as . . . ?"*
  With this type of question, the judge is attempting to apply the reasoning that you are advocating to a different, and usually less helpful, set of circumstances. By testing the soundness of your argument's logic, the judge will examine your familiarity with the material and your ability to think on your feet. The more that you have thought through your arguments, the easier you will find it to answer this sort of question. Take your time, however, and avoid suggesting a conclusion that is patently absurd.

---

[4] The steps involved in referring judges to authorities are explained in Chapter 10.

- *"Isn't there some force in your opponents' point that . . . ?"*
  Judges will commonly test mooters by putting to them points that the other side has made. Just because the judge asks you this question, it does not necessarily mean that he disagrees with your argument; it is simply another way of testing how persuasive you can be "off the cuff". Spending time before the moot thinking about how to counter your opponents' arguments will give you the edge when answering this type of question.

## "Um . . . Um . . . I don't know, My Lord"

**11–8**  Even if you have prepared meticulously for the moot and follow the practical guidance provided above, the judge may still ask you a question to which you simply do not know the answer. If you find yourself in this position, you must do your best not to let it unnerve you for the remainder of the moot. Remember that even the most eminent QCs are faced every now and then with questions that leave them scratching their heads.

When the judge asks you a question to which you do not know the answer, you still have to provide a response. And you will not have much time in which to give it. The paragraphs that follow provide a number of suggestions for how to react.

## Consult your team-mate

**11–9**  If you believe that your mooting partner may be able to answer the question, glance in his direction. A quick look should tell you whether or not he can help. If it seems that he can, and before you engage in a protracted bout of stage whispers, ask the judge for permission to consult your partner. You might do so by saying, *"My Lord, may I please briefly speak to my learned friend?"* Few judges will refuse such a request.

This strategy can work well when the judge requests information or clarification that you are unable to provide. If your mooting partner is in a position to help, the two of you will demonstrate admirable teamwork in getting to the right answer. This approach works less well, however, when the judge's intervention hits a weak spot in your argument. He will usually expect you to be able to defend your argument without first having to consult your team-mate.

## Leave the question for your team-mate to answer

**11–10**  If your team-mate has still to make his oral submissions, you can tell the judge that your partner will deal with the point during his speech. Your team-mate will then have a few minutes in which to formulate a response, which should consequently be an improvement on whatever you might come up with on the spur of the moment. This approach again works best when the judge has requested specific information or clarification that you are unable to provide.

Before telling the judge that *"my learned friend will address this point in his submissions"*, you must, of course, ensure—perhaps with a quick look over towards your team-mate or a few words with him—that he is happy to take on the task. What you cannot do is lumber your partner with responsibility for dealing with a stinker of a question when he is no better placed than you are to provide a response.

## Salvage what you can

If the judge asks a question that neither you nor your partner is able to answer, you should **11–11** nonetheless try to offer *something* positive by way of a response. Suppose, for example, that the judge asks whether you have considered the implications of a particular reported decision not cited at the moot. Although you have heard of the case, you have not read it. One option would be tell the judge point-blank, "*My Lord, I am afraid that I have not read that case and cannot therefore assist.*" This would inevitably appear rather weak. A more positive response might look like this: "*My Lord, I am not familiar with the detail of that case, but on this issue I do rely on the decision in* [refer to an authority that you *have* cited] *and my learned friends opposite have not cited any authority that undermines it.*"

This example involves a request for information, but the same principle applies if the judge's intervention hits upon a weakness in one of your arguments. If you are sufficiently conversant with the materials, you should be able to return fire, however weakly. For example, if the judge points out that your argument would lead to an unfortunate result in a particular scenario, consider whether the same result would obtain if your opponents' solution were adopted. If so, you could say to the judge, "*Your Lordship is right, but precisely the same problem arises if Your Lordship accepts the submission of my learned friends opposite.*" Your ability to make the most of a "bad lot" will, of course, develop with experience.

## Move (swiftly) on

If the judge's intervention cottons on to a weakness in your argument, you may find that, **11–12** despite your best efforts to salvage the point, the judge remains unpersuaded. In that event—which is just about your worst case scenario—there is no point in blustering. Move on to your next submission as swiftly as you can. You might do so with these words: "*My Lord, that is my submission/I cannot take this point any farther. With Your Lordship's permission, I now intend to move on to my next point.*" An implicit admission of defeat it may be, but it will at least allow you to retreat with your dignity intact.

## Summary

Some moot judges are more interventionist than others, but virtually every moot speech is **11–13** interrupted at least once by the judge. You should therefore expect interventions and prepare for them.

This chapter has considered in detail this important aspect of moot court advocacy. It has, in particular:

- Explained that the key to answering judicial questions effectively is thorough preparation.

- Discussed the practical steps that you should take whenever you answer a question from the judge.

- Listed a number of "stock" judicial questions and provided advice on how to answer them.

- Identified strategies for dealing with particularly tricky interventions.

# Organising

*"Don't agonize, organize."*

Florynce Kennedy (1916–2000)

# 12 Organising moots

**12–1** Whilst the bulk of this book is geared towards those who wish to participate in moots, this chapter is directed at those who wish to organise them. (There may, of course, be an overlap between the two.) You may, for example, be a law lecturer who wishes to set up a mooting competition as an adjunct to classes on advocacy and civil procedure. Or you may be an undergraduate law student who wants to set up a mooting society. In either event, this chapter should be of interest to you.

Organisation is vital to the success of any mooting competition. A well organised competition will generate the goodwill of the supporting institution and attract both participants and judges who will know that they are not wasting their time by taking part. In contrast, a badly organised competition tends to erode goodwill, whether of the supporting institution, the contestants or the judges, in some cases to the point where it is impossible for the competition to survive.

The extent of the assistance that you need to organise a mooting competition will, of course, depend on what, if any, arrangements you inherit. The different sections of this chapter will not therefore be relevant to everyone who sets out to organise a mooting competition. If a competition already exists at the institution where you are based, there should, for example, be little need for you to read about how to draft a set of rules. Similarly, if you are fortunate enough to have at your disposal a large number of good quality mooting problems, the section on selecting and writing moot problems may be surplus to your requirements.

## Initial considerations

**12–2** Once you have resolved to run a mooting competition, it is necessary to make some basic decisions about its organisation. In particular, you must determine how to structure it and who will be eligible to take part. A number of considerations also arise in scheduling moots. This section will examine each of these issues in turn.

### Structure of the competition

**12–3** There are two basic models for mooting competitions, which, to use a sporting analogy, may be termed "knockout" and "Champions League". The former is far more common than the latter. Both of these structures are described below, as is one of the fundamental concerns for the organiser of any mooting competition: who wins? There is then a short discussion of non-competitive or ad hoc moots.

## "Knockout" competitions

In this model, students are placed into a pyramidal draw with a series of preliminary rounds, **12–4** quarter-finals, semi-finals and a final, with the winning mooters from each "match" going through to the next round. A format for a "knockout" competition containing 16 teams is attached at Appendix II.

This format is readily understood, relatively easy to organise and motivating for students who know that they must win every round to progress. The primary disadvantage of "knockout" mooting competitions is that first-round losers do not have the opportunity to compete in a second moot unless there is some form of repechage. This can be particularly unfortunate for those, potentially able, mooters who find themselves on the wrong end of a first-round decision. The organiser of a "knockout" competition may also be faced with logistical difficulties if the number of entrants does not precisely fit the "pyramid". In those circumstances, some mooters will probably have to be given byes to the second round, which may put them at a competitive disadvantage when they have to moot against a team that has mooted before.

## "Champions League" competitions

Under this format, teams are placed into groups (usually of four) and each team moots in **12–5** successive rounds against every other team in the group. The team with the greatest number of wins then goes forward to a short "knockout" phase that concludes with the final. For anyone not familiar with this structure from European football, a diagrammatic representation is provided at Appendix III.

The major advantage of the "Champions League" format is that each team is guaranteed to moot more than once, so ensuring that the participants can focus on developing their mooting skills rather than on winning their first moot at all costs. This format is very intensive, however, in terms of the numbers of rooms and judges required because teams are not eliminated after each round. There may also be some students who do not wish to moot as many as two or three times and who will accordingly be put off by the commitment involved. From an organisational perspective, another concern is that there may be more than one team with the same number of wins after the "group stage" is completed. In that event, it will be necessary to come up with some way of deciding who goes through to the "knockout" rounds. Finally, you may run into logistical problems if the number of teams is not divisible by the number of groups, particularly as, unlike "knockout" competitions, it is not possible to grant byes.

## Who wins the moot?

Whether you adopt a "knockout" or "Champions League" format for your competition, **12–6** every moot requires a winner. You must therefore make a basic policy decision at the outset as to whether the winner will be the best team or the two best individual mooters regardless of whether or not they are on the same team.

The vast majority of mooting competitions put forward the best team and this is the only workable approach for a "Champions League" competition. Putting the best team through has a number of merits, not the least of which is that it encourages teamwork between the mooters, for example in conducting research and assisting with judicial interventions. It also mirrors professional practice, in which it is the combined efforts of the advocates acting on behalf of each party that win the day; the court does not differentiate between leading counsel for the appellant and junior counsel for the respondent.

It may nonetheless be worth at least considering the alternative of awarding the moot to the two best individual advocates. Perhaps surprisingly, some students actively encourage this approach. Their argument is usually based on the perceived unfairness of an outstanding mooter being eliminated from the competition because his or her partner is not up to scratch. This refrain is typically heard from first year law undergraduates and postgraduate students who may know very little about their chosen partners when they enter the competition. It can also be a bugbear of students who have entered the competition individually and been paired up randomly by the organiser with another lone entrant. Additionally, there is the fair point that, for those intent on entering the ranks of the profession, working with a range of different partners is a skill worth acquiring.

### Ad hoc moots

**12–7**  It is possible to organise moots on an ad hoc basis, outside the confines of a structured competition. This format can be a useful alternative if there are too few students with a sustained interest in mooting to justify a formal competition. It can also be encouraged amongst students who have been knocked out of a formal competition, but wish nevertheless to gain additional mooting experience.

The obligations on the organiser of ad hoc moots are obviously reduced. Once the participants are identified and arranged into teams, dates can be offered with "fixtures" emerging as teams declare themselves available on any given occasion. The organiser must then supply a venue, a moot problem and, of course, a judge.

The advantage of this model is its flexibility. It can accommodate students who wish to moot only once. It can also work for those mooters who have mooted before, but wish to have another go. The great disadvantage of ad hoc mooting is that students tend, unsurprisingly, to be far less motivated than when they moot in a structured competition. This can result in inconsistent levels of preparation and regular postponements.

## Eligibility to compete

**12–8**  The organiser must decide who is eligible to take part before the competition begins. There are two primary considerations to bear in mind when you make this decision: the need to ensure that there is a reasonably level playing field for all of the contestants; and the adequacy of the resources at your disposal. Both of these considerations are discussed below.

### Maintaining a level playing field

**12–9**  Most law faculties run different academic programmes that attract students of varying ages and experience. Many, for example, offer undergraduate and postgraduate law degrees, as well as postgraduate vocational courses. Some English institutions teach the Graduate Diploma in Law alongside LPC and BVC vocational courses. There is a risk that allowing students from different programmes to moot against one another will give the more experienced students a competitive advantage. In particular, students on vocational courses will usually have completed undergraduate law degrees and might therefore already have mooting experience. They will also be in the midst of a skills course that specifically teaches advocacy.

The moot organiser must decide whether these factors will render the mooting competition unfair if it is open to everyone. The selection criteria are a matter of judgment for the organiser based on the make up of the student body, the likely interest from different elements of it and the curriculum. The organiser will have to accept that there will always be an uneven playing surface to some extent. Even if eligibility is restricted to undergraduates, for example, the final-year students will enjoy an advantage over their juniors.

If the organiser takes the view that the discrepancies between the various parts of the student body will render the competition unfair if all can compete against each other, there are at least two available options. The first, if resources permit, is to run two separate competitions, one for "novices" and another for those with previous mooting experience. The second option is to restrict entry to the competition, for example by limiting it to students at a particular level (say, undergraduates other than those in their first year).

## Adequacy of resources

Mooting requires considerable resources. Every four mooters (assuming two teams of two **12–10** per moot) require a room and at least one judge for a period of as much as an hour and a half. The resources that you can bring to bear may accordingly restrict the maximum number of moots that you can run on a single night. This, in turn, is likely to affect the maximum number of students that your competition can accommodate.

You may find that the interest in your competition outstrips the resources at your disposal. In that event, you will have to impose selection criteria. There is any number of possibilities including "first come, first served", pulling names out of a hat and favouring more senior students who are in the midst of job applications and need the experience. Whichever mechanism you use, it is important to let the eligible students know as early as possible in the academic year so that you are not faced with complaints of unfairness. If resources allow, you may be able to placate disappointed students by offering them some form of ad hoc mooting.

## A strategy for limiting numbers

Students sometimes happily sign up to participate in mooting competitions without fully **12–11** appreciating what is involved. This can have a deleterious effect on the competition if swathes of participants drop out after it has started. As a moot organiser, you need to bear this risk in mind and do what you can to minimise it.

One way of impressing on students the commitment involved in mooting is to insist that all potential participants attend an initial briefing if they wish to be considered for entry into the competition. The briefing will enable you to explain in detail to students what mooting involves. Only the more motivated should then sign up for the competition with the more "flaky" potential mooters dropping by the wayside in a process of self-selection.

If you do go down this route, your briefing might include a short explanation of what mooting is and how your competition will work, a description on a task-by-task basis of what the contestants will have to do in the lead up to each moot and a word or two about the judging, identifying for example, who the judges are likely to be and the criteria that they will use to determine who wins each moot. You might round off by inviting questions from the floor and, of course, heartily recommending to those assembled that they buy a copy of this book.

## Scheduling considerations

12–12    Once you have decided on a structure for your mooting competition, you can start thinking about when each round will take place. Your schedule will have to take account of the limitations that afflict all institutions, including term dates and the availability of rooms.

It is vital when picking dates for moots to factor in the level of student workload for curricular activities. Ideally, you want to choose less intensive periods for your moots so that the students and judges have adequate time to prepare. You should also have regard to any dates for handing in assessments and try to ensure that they do not fall during the week before or the week after a moot.

## Drafting rules for mooting competitions

12–13    Whatever the structure of your competition, it will require a set of rules to give the participants the confidence that it is organised in a fair and transparent way. In any event, since mooting tends to attract the more argumentative students, it is as well to pre-empt any disagreements with a clear set of rules.

There is a specimen set of rules at Appendix IV, which you are free to adopt and modify. You may, however, want to draft a fresh set of rules to reflect your own circumstances. If you do, the following are probably the most important questions to consider:

- **Who will be eligible to take part in the competition?**
  Is it to be restricted to undergraduate students or will it be opened up to graduate students as well? Is it to be limited to a particular class of students, such as those in their final year of study? If relevant, can students on vocational courses participate?

- **The format of the competition**
  Will you employ a "knockout" or "Champions League" format? If the latter, how will you resolve any tie at the end of the group stage?

- **Who will win the moot?**
  Should the best team or the two best individual mooters win the moot?

- **Judging the moot**
  How many judges will you have for each moot? Normally, one will suffice, although you may wish to have two or three in the later rounds. You must also decide whether to have written judging criteria or whether the decision should be left entirely to the discretion of the judges. In many competitions, the judges are asked to award points to the teams based on a number of identified factors. The team (or individual mooters if this is the system that is chosen) with the greatest number of points wins the moot. If you have devised a points system, you should consider incorporating it into the competition rules. There is a sample judge's score sheet at Appendix V.

- **Skeleton arguments**

  Will the teams be obliged to produce skeleton arguments? If so, will you impose a word or page limit on each skeleton? How will you ensure that the parties exchange skeleton arguments and that you receive copies for the judge? What will the deadline for exchange be?

- **The number of authorities that each team can cite**

  Will you impose a restriction on the number of authorities that each team can cite? It is usually a good idea to do so if you are to avoid mooters submitting long lists of authorities, many of which they will be unable to refer to at the moot. If you impose a limit, you may wish to define what constitutes an authority. Will statutes, statutory instruments, textbooks and articles count? You may also wish to clarify whether cases referred to within reported decisions are themselves to count as separate authorities. This point comes up quite frequently. The sample rules in Appendix IV deal with it by explaining that the mere recitation of an extract from case B that appears in case A does not make case B an additional authority.

- **Should contestants be required to collate their authorities in a bundle?**

  The benefits of preparing bundles of authorities are discussed in Chapter 6. You may consider that those benefits are sufficient to justify requiring each team to produce a bundle in advance of every moot. The preparation of bundles does, of course, involve a certain level of added expense for the participants. Bundles are also time-consuming to produce. You might therefore consider imposing a requirement to produce a bundle only from a late stage of the competition, say the semi-final.

- **The format of authorities**

  Are you happy for the contestants to print off copies of their authorities from online databases such as Westlaw UK, LexisNexis Butterworths and Lawtel or should they be required to produce photocopies of the relevant law reports for the judge? Printing the online versions of case reports is likely to be cheaper and easier for students, but may not carry the authoritativeness or user-friendliness of a hard copy report (for example, if the submissions of counsel are missing or there are no paragraph numbers). Much will depend on the size of your competition and whether your law library stocks multiple sets of hard copy law reports.

- **Running order and timing**

  Your rules should state the order in which the mooters will speak. They should also identify the time limits on each mooter and make it clear whether those limits are inclusive or exclusive of time spent dealing with judicial interventions.

- **Reservation of powers to the competition organiser**

  You will normally want to stipulate that the organiser has the right to amend the rules and that any decision that he or she makes about the rules and their interpretation will be final.

# Obtaining sponsorship

Some mooting competitions are sponsored by local practising lawyers. Obtaining sponsorship can enhance the quality of a competition in a number of respects. First and foremost, if the competition is associated with the legal profession, it is likely to reinforce in the eyes of **12–14** the contestants how mooting can act as a bridge between education and practice; the competition is not just an offshoot of the curriculum, but has a real connection with practising the law. This tends to act as a powerful motivator for students.

Second, the sponsors are usually able to provide judges for the later rounds of the competition and possibly one or two practitioners who are prepared to give a mooting masterclass.[1] The involvement of practitioners not only provides diversity and expertise amongst the judges, it also motivates students who feel (rightly) that, if they can impress practitioner judges, they can make the grade as professional advocates.

Finally, it is likely that the sponsor will make some form of financial contribution to the competition. These funds may be used to defray the running costs of the competition or to produce a larger prize for the winners than would otherwise be possible.

## Whom to approach

**12–15**    In general, you are more likely to be successful with a local potential sponsor. Your institution may even already have a relationship with local practitioners, for example through their attending advisory panels or careers fairs. You should start with them. You should also bear in mind that there ought to be some correlation between the legal practice(s) that you approach and the likely subject matter of most of your moot problems. If, for example, your mooting competition will exclusively feature civil law problems, it may not be sensible to seek sponsorship from a law firm that only practises criminal law.

## How to approach potential sponsors

**12–16**    It is important that you explain clearly and succinctly to potential sponsors what you are looking for as well as the advantages to them in getting involved. You might start by producing a short letter summarising three key points: how the competition will work; what you would like from the sponsor; and what you perceive to be the advantages to the sponsor. Set out below is a little more detail about the sort of information that you could include on each of these three points.

### How the competition will work

You might explain how many students are involved in the competition, the academic programme (or programmes) that those students are undertaking, the proposed structure of the competition and any key organisational features (such as whether skeleton arguments are required). Information of this nature should impress on potential sponsors that your mooting competition is well organised and worthy of support.

### What you would like from the sponsor

Your wish list is likely to include some or all of the following: use of the sponsor's name on promotional materials; a cash sum to contribute towards the running costs and/or prizes;

---

[1] Masterclasses are discussed later in this chapter.

possibly, a prize in the form of a guaranteed spot on a vacation placement or mini-pupillage scheme; the provision of judges for the later rounds of the competition; and a commitment to conduct a mooting masterclass.

### The advantages to the sponsor

Most practitioners are only too aware of the need to market themselves effectively to students with a view to optimising their recruitment programmes. Involvement in mooting can enable practitioners to put themselves across in a more focused and interactive fashion than at a formal marketing event. The opportunities are greatest if there is going to be a pre-moot masterclass or a post-moot social gathering or prize-giving.

# Publicising mooting competitions

Publicity can play an important part in the success of a mooting competition. Before the **12–17** competition is launched, the role of publicity is to inform students of its existence and to encourage as many students as possible to sign up. Once the competition is up and running, the primary object of publicity is to maximise the number of spectators at each moot. Good publicity, whether before or after the competition has started, will raise the profile of the competition within the institution and attract the interest of students who are not directly involved. They may come along to watch moots out of curiosity or to support friends who are taking part. Well judged publicity can also create a "feel good" factor around the mooting competition, bringing it into the mainstream of student life.

## Pre-launch publicity

A poster campaign is the most obvious way of raising awareness amongst students before a **12–18** mooting competition gets under way. It is often more effective to use your posters to promote a message suggestive of what mooting is about (such as persuasion or verbal duelling) than to rely on an anodyne "*would you like to join the mooting society?*" A specimen pre-launch poster appears in Appendix VI.

If your finances permit, you should consider producing a short brochure that you can distribute to all interested students at the freshers' fair and elsewhere. The brochure might explain briefly what mooting is and what its benefits are, provide details of the structure of the competition that you have organised and the dates on which moots will take place, and explain what further steps students need to take if they wish to sign up. You will find sample text for such a brochure at Appendix VII.

To ensure maximum coverage, it is advisable to ask lecturers either to make an announcement or to show a publicity slide at the start of their classes. Additionally, if your institution has a newsletter or intranet, do not pass up the opportunity to advertise there. If you are beginning to feel uneasy that this approach has more in common with ambush marketing than restrained academic publicity, rest assured that, no matter how hard you try, there will always be some students who complain that they were not made aware at the start of the term that they could moot.

## Post-launch publicity

**12–19**   The role of publicity after the competition is in train is principally to advertise when and where each moot is taking place, and to make it clear that spectators are welcome. A sample post-launch poster appears in Appendix VIII. It has been used to advertise a post-graduate mooting competition. The black and white lines, and the slightly cryptic message certainly served to get it noticed.

   When advertising the dates and locations of moots, you might consider making use of whatever student newsletter your institution runs. Your publicity might also mention the names of the contestants and judges, and the subject matter of the moot (e.g. contract or tort/delict). You could even reproduce the whole moot problem if you have space.

## Selecting and briefing the judges

**12–20**   The quality of the judging and, in particular, of the feedback that the judges give to the mooters is integral to the success of a mooting competition. It is therefore critical to put some time and effort into selecting and briefing the judges involved in your competition.

## Selecting judges

**12–21**   There are broadly three categories of judges: students; members of the academic staff at your institution; and practitioners. Each category is discussed below.

### Students

**12–22**   Unless you are running a very small mooting competition, it is likely that you will make some use of students as judges. For many competitions, they will be the most common source of judicial material.

   The principal advantage of student judges is their availability. Many students, particularly ex-mooters, are only too happy to subject their peers to judicial scrutiny. Availability is not the only advantage of student judges, however. They will usually understand more acutely than other types of judge what the participants are going through. They are accordingly often able to provide perceptive and comprehensible feedback.

   The principal drawback of student judges is that they tend to lack the gravitas of academics and practitioners. As a result, there is a danger of the proceedings becoming too relaxed and informal.

### Members of the academic staff

**12–23**   Using academics as judges has a number of advantages. As long as you are able to match the right members of staff to the right moots, they will have considerable knowledge of the subject area, which should facilitate some good interventions. Most members of staff are also able to adopt sufficient judicial airs to ensure that the moot is conducted with the requisite degree of seriousness. The flip-side of this is that some mooters find it difficult to adjust to members of the academic staff acting as judges. Some may even be concerned about performing in front of people who might be marking their exams at the end of the year.

None of this should dissuade you from using members of staff as judges. Indeed, the drawbacks referred to above are not dissimilar to the difficulties that advocates sometimes face in practice when they find themselves appearing before judges who were formerly colleagues. The one real disadvantage of calling on academics to act as judges is that their hours of work and domestic commitments may mean that they are not always available to judge in the evening, when most moots take place.

## Practitioners

The most obvious advantage of using practitioners as judges is that they bring with them **12–24** professional experience of the judicial process. They know how judges act and the feedback that they give will satisfy the desire of the participants to know how things are done in practice. One downside of using practitioners to judge your moots is that they tend to be even less available than members of staff and therefore need to be used more sparingly. It can also be quite intimidating for students to face practitioner judges. They are therefore generally best employed in the later rounds of mooting competitions.

Practitioners, of course, hail from a wide variety of backgrounds. The particular expertise of any given practitioner will to some extent govern what he or she brings to the mooting experience. The most obvious distinctions between practitioners are described below:

- **Judge or advocate**
  Practising judges are clearly the best people to give definitive guidance on what does or does not persuade them. They often pick up on points that other types of moot judge are less concerned about, such as what to wear in court. The fortes of practising advocates, by contrast, are to guide students on how to prepare their cases, to explain the tricks of the advocate's trade and to prepare students for the different styles of judging that they are likely to encounter in practice.

- **Criminal or civil advocate**
  Criminal advocates spend the majority of their working lives on their feet in court. As a result of this, and of the "blood and guts" nature of their practices, they usually have a fund of excellent tips for effective advocacy as well as a plethora of interesting courtroom "war stories". Although civil advocates are generally less well versed in the art of examining witnesses, they often have more experience of drafting skeleton arguments and making submissions on the law, both of which are key mooting skills.

- **Senior or junior advocate**
  Senior advocates bring gravitas and experience to judging, but their very seniority can distance them from the average mooter. Junior advocates provide a closer reference point and students can usually relate to them more easily. They are also more likely to appear regularly in the types of court where mooters will begin their professional careers.

- **Advocate or litigation solicitor**
  Litigation solicitors who do not themselves appear in court usually still have a well developed sense of what to look for in an advocate, as well as a good stock of

advocacy anecdotes. The principal disadvantage of using litigation solicitors as judges is that they will not be able to tell mooters how they would themselves deal with a particular point or difficulty.

# Briefing judges

12–25   Whether your judges are students, academics or practitioners, it is important that you brief them adequately on how you want them to approach their task. A sensible option is to send your judges copies of a short written guidance note in advance of the moot. Appendix IX contains sample text for such a note. The note that you draft will, of course, have to reflect the rules of your competition. If you decide to write a briefing note from scratch, you should ensure that it covers the topics discussed below.

## The system for judging

12–26   You will have to explain to the judges the system that you have chosen to determine the winners of the moot. If you have devised a points system, for example, your briefing note should identify each category that you are asking the judges to score, the maximum number of points available under each head and how many points you would award for excellent, good, average and poor performances. Without this latter indication, some judges may be naturally meaner or more generous than others when scoring. Maintaining consistency will then be very difficult.

## The principal rules of the competition

12–27   You should draw the judges' attention in the briefing note to the most significant of the competition rules. Two good examples are the speaking time allotted to each mooter (making it clear whether this is exclusive or inclusive of time spent dealing with judicial interventions) and the maximum number of authorities on which each mooter is entitled to rely. You might also include some generic advice on how to deal with breaches of the rules by the participants. You could explain, for example, how the judges should deal with common defaults such as mooters running over their allotted speaking time or attempting to introduce authorities that have not been notified in advance of the moot.

## Guidelines on judicial interventions

12–28   Intervention is a key area. If there is not enough of it, the moot becomes little more than a presentation and lacks the authenticity of the courtroom experience. Too much intervention and the moot can take on the aura of an exchange with the Spanish Inquisition. In order to strike a happy medium, you should consider advising judges to think about the following points when intervening:

- **Test the submission not the law**
  The intervention should generally test the argument that the mooter makes rather than the mooter's wider knowledge of the law. For example, an intervention to the effect that, *"if you take that submission to its logical conclusion, does it not mean [X]?"* is fairer than an intervention along the lines of, *"do you know of any other reported case in this area of the law that supports your submission?"*.

- **Ask each mooter roughly the same number of questions**
  Each mooter should be subjected to approximately the same number of interventions. Save, perhaps, in the later rounds of the competition, when the mooters can reasonably expect to face more searching questions from the bench, judges should think in terms of making two or three significant interventions per mooter.

- **Do not labour the point**
  Whilst mooters should be given every opportunity to answer questions from the bench, if they are obviously floundering, judges should encourage them to move on to another point. Although being moved along in this way can be a bit of a blow to the mooter's confidence, it is generally more palatable for all concerned (not least the audience) than an embarrassed and prolonged silence.

## Guidelines on giving judgment

In the context of mooting, giving judgment is a two-stage process: a judgment on the law and **12–29** a judgment on the moot. Judges should be guided on both.

- **Judgment on the law**
  The judgment on the law should be short, but reasoned. Given the amount of time that the contestants will have devoted to the moot problem, they are entitled to expect a sensible judgment. Some of the audience will also be interested in the rationale for the legal outcome. If there are going to be multiple judges on the moot bench, you might even suggest that one of them gives a short dissenting judgment. It can certainly add an element of levity to the proceedings.

- **Judgment on the moot**
  Strictly speaking, the judgment on the moot is no more than the bare statement that one team (or two mooters) has won. It should, however, also include feedback on the strengths and weaknesses of the individual participants. Some judges prefer to announce who has won the moot before going on to give individual feedback. Others take the reverse approach. Either way works well, although waiting until the end to announce the result does have the advantage of ensuring that both teams listen attentively to the feedback.

## Guidelines on giving feedback

Many students emphasise that it is the feedback that most helps them to reflect on their **12–30** performances and improve their mooting skills. It is therefore important that your judges are well briefed on giving feedback. It may be worth, in particular, warning them to avoid either of the two extreme models for giving feedback. At the "right-wing" extreme are those judges who give a fully itemised breakdown of every error that each mooter made, from typos in the skeleton arguments to failing to wear a sufficiently conservative tie. At the "left-wing" extreme are those judges who favour generalised "pat on the back" feedback along the lines of, *"both teams were very good, but team B was slightly better"*.

Neither of these extremes will help the mooters to improve. In order to achieve that objective, consider advising your judges to think about the following when giving feedback:

- **Focus on a small number of points**
  Judges should restrict themselves to no more than two or three points of feedback. They should concentrate on those issues that will make the greatest difference to the overall standard of performance.

- **Start with positive feedback**
  Judges should begin their feedback by giving an example of something that the mooter did well, rather than a biting criticism.

- **Give examples of problem areas and suggest solutions**
  Negative feedback is generally the most valuable, but it must be handled with care. It can often assist if the judges are able to provide concrete examples of the errors that the mooters made. Having criticised a mooter's performance, a judge should always suggest how it could have been improved. The judge might say, for example, that, *"You became confused about how to address the bench. You might try writing out the appropriate mode of address at the top of each page of your notes so that you always have it in front of you when you are speaking."*

# Mooting masterclasses

**12–31**   Masterclasses are most often associated with the world of music, when distinguished musicians give advanced instruction on one or two selected compositions to eager audiences of students. In mooting terms, the purpose of a masterclass is very similar. An experienced practitioner, supported by the organiser of the mooting competition, seeks to develop specific mooting skills through a mixture of demonstration and critique.

Mooting masterclasses can take many forms, right up to a full mock moot between students or practitioners. It is important, however, that any masterclass that you run is pitched at an appropriate level that reflects how much your students know about mooting.

Two types of masterclass are described below: (1) an introduction to mooting; and, (2) a more advanced lesson in specific mooting skills. Both are mere examples. Any number of other topics may fit the bill.

## Introductory masterclass

**12–32**   The purpose of an introductory masterclass is to explain in general terms what mooting involves. It might therefore take place before the first round of your mooting competition begins. Events of this type can be an excellent opportunity for junior practitioners to recount their own experiences and to emphasise how mooting helped them in practice. In many cases, practitioners are also happy to emphasise how mooting can assist students with job applications.

An introductory masterclass might include a straightforward interactive exercise, which gives students a flavour of what mooting involves as well as some guidance and feedback on the basic skills required. An example exercise of this sort is described in figure 12.1.

An exercise of this sort reflects the common mooting scenario in which the judge asks the mooter for a summary of the salient facts of a cited case. The exercise forces the students to focus on the central facts of the decision. It also puts them through the experience (in some cases for the first time) of listening to the sound of their own voices when making legal submissions in front of an audience.

## Figure 12.1: Introductory masterclass

12–33

At the beginning of the masterclass, distribute the headnote from a well-known reported case and tell the students that they have five minutes to read it and make notes about it. Once the time expires, ask for volunteers to stand up and, in no more than one minute, summarise the facts of the case to the practitioner. The students should be told to address their remarks to the practitioner as if he or she were a judge.

After each student's submissions, the practitioner should provide some brief feedback, concentrating in particular on stance, voice projection, eye contact and the appropriate use of language.

# Advanced masterclass

The aim of an advanced masterclass is to give students practical assistance in developing one or more higher level mooting skills. It typically takes place after the first round of a mooting competition, by which point the participants should already be familiar with the basics of mooting.   **12–34**

There is a wide variety of topics that you can use for an advanced masterclass. You could opt, for example, for a masterclass on devising an efficient research strategy or on dealing effectively with judicial interventions. You should generally choose the subject matter jointly with the practitioner who leads the masterclass since the professional background of your practitioner is likely to determine how he or she can best add value.

One possibility for an advanced masterclass is the effective use of skeleton arguments and authorities during oral submissions. These are two areas in which mooters often struggle and where practitioners can add real value. Set out in figure 12.2 is an example exercise of such a masterclass based on the illustrative case of *Cecil v Dickens*.

## Figure 12.2: Advanced masterclass

12–35

A week or so before the masterclass is due to take place, distribute to the likely attendees copies of the moot problem in *Cecil v Dickens* together with short specimen skeleton arguments on behalf of both of the parties. The skeletons should deal with only one of the grounds of appeal and will have been drafted either by you or by the practitioner leading the masterclass. Ask the students to read the moot problem, the skeleton arguments and one of the reported cases cited in one of the skeleton arguments, and to prepare in advance of the masterclass a two-minute submission based on those materials for one side or the other. You should explain that the submission will be made to the practitioner, as if he or she were a judge, and that it must refer both to the relevant passage of the skeleton argument and to at least one passage from the reported case.

During the masterclass, volunteers should be sought to make submissions. It should be at the practitioner's discretion whether or not to intervene with questions. After each student has completed his submissions, the practitioner should provide brief feedback, focusing on how effectively the student managed to link the skeleton argument and the authority. The practitioner should also be prepared to give a short demonstration at the end of the session showing how he or she would make the same submission in practice.

# General considerations for organising masterclasses

There are three particular organisational considerations that you should bear in mind when organising masterclasses (whether introductory or advanced):   **12–36**

- **Timing and attendees**
  You should schedule each masterclass to last for an hour and a half at most. This is, frankly, the limit of most students' attention spans. Provided that there is space to accommodate them, consider extending the invitation to all interested students rather than just those who are eligible to take part in the mooting competition.

- **Publicity**
  To ensure maximum attendance, make sure that you publicise the masterclass appropriately. The same publicity machine that you employed to get the mooting competition noticed in the first place[2] can also be wheeled into action for this purpose.

- **The social element**
  You should ascertain in advance whether the practitioner giving the masterclass is free to stay on afterwards. If so, consider laying on a reception of some sort. It need not be lavish, but it can provide an important opportunity for the practitioner to speak to the students on an informal basis and to clarify one-to-one any specific points that students wish to raise.

# Logistics in the run-up to the moot

**12–37** By this stage, you will have the structure of your competition in place, you will have arranged the dates and locations of the early round moots, and the contestants will have been suitably enthused by the introductory masterclass that you have provided. You will even have a cadre of willing judges lined up and ready to jump into action. There is still a bit to do before the night of the first moot, however. Three particular tasks are discussed below: creating a communication network; devising a pre-moot timetable; and facilitating the exchange of authorities and skeleton arguments.

## Creating a communication network

**12–38** For the first round of a sizeable mooting competition, you might have 100 people or more involved as mooters, judges and court clerks. Before the moots kick off, you therefore need to devise an efficient system of communicating with them and for them to communicate with each other (for example, to exchange skeleton arguments and lists of authorities). Noticeboards are the time-honoured means of conveying information in most institutions. In the electronic age, however, there are more sophisticated options available. In particular, you might be able to produce a group e-mail with all of those involved as recipients. With one click of your mouse, you will then be able to let them know what is happening, where and when. An added advantage of compiling a group e-mail is that it will give you a preliminary list of contact details when it comes to arranging judging and gaining other assistance for the following year's competition.

---

[2] See the discussion of publicity earlier in this chapter.

You might also consider constructing an Excel spreadsheet that sets out who is taking part in each moot and lists everyone's contact details. Colour-coding can make the spreadsheet more user-friendly. Having created a spreadsheet, you could disseminate it in hard copy or electronically. The participants should then have all of the information that they need to make contact with each other.

## Pre-moot timetable

It is essential to devise a timetable that you and the moot participants must adhere to in the **12–39** build-up to each moot. Although the precise steps contained in any given timetable will vary from competition to competition, each should provide, at the very least, for the distribution of the moot problem (the organiser's responsibility) and the exchange of authorities and skeleton arguments (the mooters' responsibility). The timetable should be provided as early as possible to all those involved. An example timetable is set out in table 12.3.

### Table 12.3: Pre-Moot timetable

| Step | Deadline |
|---|---|
| The organiser sends a group e-mail to all mooters and judges attaching a spreadsheet with the participants' names and contact details, as well as details of the location and timing of each moot. | M(oot)-21 days |
| The organiser distributes the moot problem to the mooters and judges. | M-14 days |
| The mooters exchange lists or bundles of the authorities on which they intend to rely and provide copies to the organiser. If required by the competition rules, the mooters also exchange skeleton arguments and provide copies to the organiser for transmission to the judge. | M-2 days |

**12–40**

## Exchange of authorities and skeleton arguments

The last element of your pre-moot timetable is the deadline by which the mooters must **12–41** exchange the authorities on which they intend to rely and any skeleton arguments. In order to mimic practice, it is generally desirable for contestants to exchange authorities at the same time as their skeleton arguments. This should give both the judges and the mooters a sufficient opportunity to read the material in detail prior to the moot.

You will need to decide how exchange is going to take place. You might leave it to the mooters to arrange exchange between themselves and to drop off with you one copy of each document for the judge. Alternatively, you may have to act as a post box through which the mooters exchange their authorities and skeleton arguments. Although this latter course will involve more work for you, it is more likely to ensure that both sides adhere to the required timetable.

# Day of the moot

**12–42** The role of the moot organiser on the day of the moot is not dissimilar to that of a "front of house" manager in a theatre. You are the public face of the competition and must troubleshoot any problems that arise. At the same time, you cannot dictate the outcome of the proceedings. That is down to the "cast"—the mooters and judges. What you can do, however, is ensure that they have the optimum conditions in which to perform.

The organiser has a number of important tasks to undertake on the day of the moot. Each of them is described briefly below.

## Setting up the moot courtroom

**12–43** As described in Chapter 8, moot courtrooms are arranged in a particular way that reflects the lay-out of real-life courtrooms. You will need to ensure that the rooms in which your moots take place are set up along similar lines. As well as arranging the tables and chairs, you should give some consideration to the following:

- **Seating for the audience**
  You will need to make sure that there are sufficient chairs in the room to accommodate spectators. It can be difficult to gauge the likely size of the audience, although the later rounds inevitably attract greater numbers. It is generally better to have too many chairs than too few. Moots that are "standing room only" (believe it or not, they do occasionally happen) may generate the atmosphere of a high-profile libel trial, but you will not endear yourself to the poor souls who have to remain on their feet for an hour or more. You might also consider printing off copies of the moot problem and making them available to the spectators as they arrive. They should, as a result, find it easier to follow the submissions and engage with the moot.

- **Lecterns**
  If possible, you should provide at least one lectern for each moot courtroom. Ideally, you will have one per team so that the mooters are not obliged to pass the lectern to each other between speeches. It is possible to improvise if you are faced with a lectern shortage. You might, for example, provide a despatch box that will give the mooters a reasonable platform for their papers.

- **Water**
  It is customary to provide a jug of water and glasses both for the mooters and for the judge. The water may be left untouched, but it can be a godsend if one of the participants develops a hacking cough mid-speech.

- **Notices**
  Consider putting a notice on the door of each moot courtroom that identifies the names of the mooters and the judge, as well as the relevant round of the competition. Not only will this help the participants and the spectators to work out where they should be, it may even help you.

# Briefing the moot court clerk

Since mooting competitions invariably impose limits on the speaking time allotted to each **12–44** mooter, you need to ensure that someone is charged with keeping track of the length of each mooter's submissions. This need is especially acute when the rules of the competition provide that the speaking time allotted to each mooter is exclusive of time spent dealing with judicial interventions since the watch needs to be stopped and started with considerable regularity. Although judges can take on this role, it is preferable to enlist the services of a student volunteer to act as a court clerk. His or her responsibilities need not be limited to timing the submissions, of course. Court clerks can also act as conduits for the mooters to pass any papers up to the judge (or, rarely, *vice versa*) and can assist in setting up the moot courtroom.

If you do employ the services of court clerks, you should brief them on the day of the moot. You should tell them how to time the mooters' submissions and you should explain any mechanism that you have devised for letting the mooters know how much time they have left. The least intrusive method is probably for the court clerk to display a flash card at various intervals; for example, once when a minute remains and again when time is up. An alternative is to use a buzzer or bell, although the noise involved can throw mooters off their stride.

# Meeting the judge before the moot begins

Once the judge has arrived, the organiser should have a quick word with him. The discussion **12–45** should cover the following areas in particular:

- **Documents**
  The organiser should check that the judge has a copy of the moot problem, the authorities relied on by each team, the parties' skeleton arguments (if any), the competition rules, any criteria for judging and giving feedback, and any briefing note that you distributed in advance of the moot.

- **Timing of submissions**
  The organiser should explain how the mooters' submissions will be timed. If a court clerk is going to be employed, it may be sensible to introduce him or her to the judges.

- **Choosing a division of labour**
  If there is more than one judge, the organiser might suggest that they divide the labour between them, particularly the tasks of making judicial interventions and jotting down the notes that will form the basis for evaluating the mooters' performances.

- **Questions**
  It is always worthwhile asking judges whether they have any questions, particularly regarding issues that commonly arise during moots such as the appropriate time limits for the mooters' submissions and the rules on judicial interventions. Organisers should also mention that they or one of their assistants will be available to advise on any particular points that arise.

# Assisting the judge when deliberating

12–46    Once the mooters have concluded their submissions, most judges will want to deliberate before announcing a decision. You should generally invite judges to retire to another room. If there is nowhere else to go, at least make sure that any discussion between multiple judges takes place outside the earshot of the competitors and spectators.

As a judge begins to deliberate, you should check whether any guidance is required. The most common areas of concern tend to be those identified below.

### Separating two closely matched teams

The judge may tell you that the moot was extremely closely fought and that he or she is struggling to distinguish between the teams. In those circumstances, you should suggest that the judge focuses on the key skills identified in the competition rules and in any judging criteria that you have produced. Typically, for example, judges will be asked to give particular weight to the abilities of the mooters to deal effectively with judicial interventions. They might, alternatively, lay particular emphasis on the skeleton arguments or on teamwork. Even in very tight contests, there will be objective ways of distinguishing between the contestants. What the organiser should, of course, avoid is attempting to influence the decision.

### Dealing with an unbalanced team

In mooting competitions where the best team goes through, judges will sometimes tell you that one team contained both the outstanding individual mooter and the weakest mooter on show. Who, then, should win?

The only advice that you can give in those circumstances is that the judge must advance the best overall team even if that results in the outstanding individual bowing out of the competition. Judges can, of course, emphasise in their feedback how impressed they were by a particular performance. They should be wary of over-doing it, however, given the implication that the team would have won had the best individual's partner been half-competent.

### Dealing with breaches of the rules

Judges sometimes ask what they should do about a team that consists of the better mooters, but commits some breach of the rules (typically speaking for too long). The best counsel for the organiser is generally to tell the judge to award the moot to the best team as long as the other side was not materially prejudiced by the breach of the rules. A team might be sufficiently prejudiced, for example, if its opponents failed to serve a skeleton argument in advance of the moot.

# After the moot

12–47    As each round of your mooting competition finishes and the dust settles, there are two principal tasks that you should consider undertaking (in addition to breathing a deep sigh of relief).

## Arranging publicity for the winners

It is always a good idea to publicise the winners of each round of moots. This not only serves **12–48** to validate the students' efforts, it also increases the profile of the competition. Publicity might take the form of an announcement on noticeboards around the institution or in the student newspaper. You will probably want to engage in more elaborate publicity for the overall winners of the competition. Some institutions will, for example, hang photographs of past winners in the law library. There might even be a short presentation by the dean of the faculty.

## Enlisting contestants to help with future competitions

As this year's competition draws to a close, you should be looking towards next year's event. **12.49** Two particular questions should be at the forefront of your mind: who will organise the next competition; and who will act as judges? You can go some way towards easing both concerns by recruiting as many as possible of this year's crop of mooters to help organise and judge next year's competition.

In the case of students who are graduating, it is particularly important to retain their details on file, so that you can track them down in future years and ask them to return as judges. There are few things more satisfying for a moot organiser than introducing past graduates of your mooting competition as practitioner judges. For those competitors who are about to graduate, it is a good idea to bombard them fairly early on with requests to act as judges in coming years. It often makes a big difference if you ask people to help when the positive experience of mooting remains fresh in their minds. If you leave it until the start of the next academic year, your judging pool may have developed other interests.

## Selecting and writing moot problems

Choosing the right moot problem is an essential part of organising a moot. Get it right and **12–50** even the most pedestrian contestants will find good points to make. Get it wrong and the most talented of mooters will struggle.

You have two principal choices when deciding on your moot problem. The first is to select an existing problem and either use it as it is or modify it in some way. The second is to write your own, original moot problem.

## Using existing moot problems

If your mooting competition is well established, the chances are that your predecessors will **12–51** have bequeathed you a stock of moot problems. If you are not in this fortunate position or are simply on the look out for new problems, there are several sources of moot problems in the public domain. In most cases, the authors make it clear that they are happy for their problems to be reproduced.

## *Where to find existing moot problems*

**12–52** There are two principal sources of existing moot problems: textbooks and the internet. This text provides the illustrative problem of *Cecil v Dickens* as well as the specimen problems of *Huggins v Hobdell* and *Smith v Designer Fashions Limited*, which are at Appendices X and XI respectively. Kaye and Townley's, *Blackstone's Book of Moots* contains a large number of sample moot problems. It is now more than ten years old, however, so you will need to make sure that the law has not changed in any respect that might materially affect the problem that you select.

There are also numerous websites from which you can download sample moot problems. They include *www.mootingnet.org.uk, www.oup.co.uk/oxfordtextbooks/law/mooting/more* and *www.essexcourt.net/esu.* Needless to say, you should always carry out your own due diligence before using any publicly-available problem for one of your moots.

## *Selecting existing moot problems*

**12–53** Not all moot problems are created equal. It is therefore important to have regard to a few basic questions when assessing the suitability of someone else's moot problem for your mooting competition. In particular, you should ask the following questions:

- **Does the moot problem offer credible arguments for both sides?**
  There are two common situations in which this may not be so. The first is where the moot problem is old and there has been a subsequent change in the law that provides a definitive answer to all or part of the problem. The second is where the problem was poorly drafted in the first place and excessively favoured one side over the other.

- **Will the moot problem involve too much research?**
  Research is, of course, an integral part of mooting. But it is important that the depth of research required is not such that the participants are unable to do justice to themselves without spending untold hours in the law library. If that is what happens, your competition may haemorrhage participants. As a general rule of thumb, try to ensure that at least one of the grounds of appeal that the problem raises lies within an area of law that the contestants have already studied as part of the curriculum. This will not prevent the contestants from having to carry out further research, as it is unlikely that they will have covered the point in sufficient depth for mooting purposes, but it does mean that they will be refining their knowledge rather than researching the problem from first principles.

- **Does the problem reflect the stage that the competition has reached?**
  For a first round moot, relatively straightforward problems dealing, for example, with offer and acceptance in contract or liability in negligence tend to work best. More esoteric topics, such as nuisance, occupiers' liability or human rights law, may be appropriate in the later stages of the competition. Of course, the difficulty of the problem is not necessarily linked to the area of law with which it is concerned. Some negligence problems, for example, raise exceptionally complicated issues of law and policy.

- **Is the problem realistic?**
  There is a view that realism does not matter and that the facts of moot problems can be ludicrously far-fetched. However, many students respond poorly to scenarios that seem to have more in common with the plot of an Ealing comedy than with the sort

of cases that actually play out in the courts. You may also cause problems if the names of the fictitious parties are so amusing that they become a distraction at the moot itself. Whilst a degree of unreality is inevitable, it is best to choose problems that are based on factual scenarios that might arise in real life.

## Tips for modifying existing moot problems

You may find that you like the basic scenario of an existing moot problem, but are not **12–54** completely satisfied that it meets your requirements. You might then look to modify it. Although the precise modifications that you make will obviously depend on the deficiencies that you perceive in the original problem, there are two particular tweaks that you might consider making:

- **Expanding the findings of fact of the trial judge**
  Some moot problems, particularly in the realms of contract and tort/delict, do not make it clear whether the trial judge made a finding on causation. This can leave the contestants free to argue the point, which they often do with mixed results. If you come across a moot problem of this sort, you might wish to add particular findings on causation to avoid the mooters from speculating about what the trial judge held.

- **Adding a cross-appeal**
  If the moot problem heavily favours one side, you might add a cross-appeal that leans the other way and thereby makes the problem more evenly balanced. If, for example, you have found a negligence problem in which the trial judge decided that a duty of care arose, but gave judgment for the defendant on the basis that there was no causation and that the loss was too remote, you might add a cross-appeal against the judge's findings on breach of duty.

# How to write your own moot problems

Although adopting or modifying an existing moot problem can produce perfectly satisfactory **12–55** results, there are advantages to writing your own. As well as producing a hard-to-rival sense of intellectual satisfaction, you can tailor the problem to fit the dictates of the participants' curriculum or to highlight particular issues of interest.

There are several starting-points for writing moot problems. Three of them are briefly discussed below.

## Using "hot topics" as a starting-point

The most fruitful source of new moot problems tends to be those areas of the law (so-called **12–56** "hot topics") that are generally acknowledged to be intractable or developing, or that have given rise to conflicting judgments in the higher courts. The following are examples of current "hot topics":

**Contract law**

- Whether an advertisement amounts to a contractually-binding offer or a mere invitation to treat. The leading case is still *Carlill v Carbolic Smokeball Co*.[3] This is an

---

[3] [1893] 1 QB 256.

old favourite and a sample moot problem that deals with this area of the law (*Smith v Designer Fashions Limited*) is contained in Appendix XI.

- Breach of contract claims in which the party in breach relies on an exclusion clause. These cases lend themselves to moot problems with two grounds of appeal, the first being whether the exclusion clause was incorporated into the contract and the second whether, if so, it satisfied the statutory test of reasonableness.[4]

**Tort**

- Whether a duty of care in negligence exists to avoid pure economic loss. This is the issue raised by the first ground of appeal in the illustrative problem of *Cecil v Dickens*.

- Whether it is necessary to have a proprietary interest in land in order to found a claim in private nuisance. The specimen moot problem at Appendix X entitled *Huggins v Hobdell* deals with this issue.

- The circumstances in which a secondary victim can recover damages for nervous shock. A variation on this theme is whether a victim can recover damages for nervous shock after damage to property, say in the aftermath of a burglary.

**Criminal law**

- What constitutes "property" and "belonging to another" under section 15(1) of the Theft Act 1968. Does this provision cover, for example, a situation in which someone lies about his address in order to get his child into a school for which he was not, in fact, eligible?

- The distinction between *mens rea* and *actus reus*. An example of this type of problem that is sometimes employed as an interview scenario for intending law students is the situation where a wife attempts to kill her husband (or *vice versa* if you prefer) by deliberately poisoning his supper. She mistakenly confuses the poison with harmless white powder and the husband survives the meal. The wife then makes her husband a cup of tea and inadvertently adds the poison, believing it to be sugar. She consequently succeeds in killing him this time, but without meaning to. The "moot point" is whether the jury can properly be directed to convict the wife of murder in circumstances where the *actus reus* and the *mens rea* of the offence do not coincide.

**EU law**

- Whether a state-imposed advertising restriction on a particular product constitutes a "measure having equivalent effect" and, if so, whether the member state can justify it under Article 30 or Article 56 of the EU Treaty. For a consideration of these issues by the European Court of Justice, see case C-405/98 *Konsumentombudsmannen v Gourmet International Products AB*,[5] which concerned Sweden's ban on alcohol advertising.

**Land law**

- Whether a particular arrangement constitutes a lease or a licence.

- How to resolve the competing claims of the finder of lost property and the owner of the land on which it was found.

---

[4] Under the Unfair Contract Terms Act 1977 and/or the European regulation.
[5] [2001] All ER (EC) 308.

**Public law**

- The extent to which Article 9 of the ECHR protects every act motivated or inspired by a religion or belief. This issue is dealt with in the specimen moot problem of *Huggins v Hobdell* at Appendix X.

- Whether breach of a particular statute gives rise to an action by an individual for breach of statutory duty.

**Scots law**

- Whether, if an innocent party purchases property that the seller acquired by fraud, the sale contract is voidable or void.

- Whether it is sufficient in order to establish a defence to a charge of rape for the accused to prove that he genuinely believed that the victim consented or whether he must also show that his belief was based on reasonable grounds.

## *Using an old seminar or exam question as a starting-point*

You may be able to find problem questions that have been used in seminars or exams that, **12–57** with a little modification, can make effective moot problems. Your primary considerations in hunting for appropriate problem questions are likely to be the subject-matter with which they are concerned and the complexity of the issues that they raise. The best moot problems are generally concerned with mainstream areas of the law and concentrate on a small number of legal issues.

Once you have identified a seminar or exam question that you believe might fit the bill, you should rework it into moot problem format. This is likely to involve the following alterations:

- **Limiting the parties and causes of action**
  A moot problem should usually be concerned with a single piece of litigation, not multiple claims involving manifold parties. If the seminar or exam question that you are using addresses numerous claims, rework it to excise all but one.

- **Creating a judgment of the lower court**
  Seminar and exam questions normally recite a factual scenario, but not in the form of a judgment. By contrast, a moot problem requires a lower court judgment in order to set up an appeal. However, you can readily turn the factual scenario in a seminar or exam question into the lower court's findings of fact.

- **Drafting the grounds of appeal**
  Moot problems need grounds of appeal, which seminar and exam questions never have. In most cases, you can simply make the grounds of appeal the opposite of whatever you have stated were the findings of the trial judge. If the judge held, for example, that "*the defendant did not provide consideration for the claimant's promise*", the ground of appeal would be that, "*the Learned Judge erred in law in finding that the defendant did not provide good consideration for the claimant's promise*". Since Scots law does not require consideration, this ground of appeal would plainly not work for a moot north of the Border.

## *Using an appellate court decision as a starting-point*

A further method for drafting moot problems is to find a recent appeal court decision that **12–58** contains either a dissenting judgment or a judgment in which the judge suggested that, had the facts been slightly different, he would have reached a contrary conclusion. You can then design a moot problem in which the facts are changed either to raise more starkly the dissenting judge's concerns or specifically to include the facts contemplated by the "differing" judge.

This process can be illustrated briefly by the decision of the House of Lords in *Hunter v Canary Wharf Limited*,[6] which overruled the Court of Appeal in finding that the erection of a tall building that interfered with local residents' television reception did not give the residents an actionable claim in private nuisance. By the time the case reached the House of Lords, it raised two legal issues: whether interference with television reception is capable of constituting an actionable nuisance; and whether it is necessary to have an interest in property to claim in private nuisance. Lord Cooke dissented on the second of these issues (the majority of the House of Lords found that a property interest is a prerequisite of bringing a claim). This second issue accordingly offers scope for use in a moot problem.

If you were to use *Hunter* as the basis for a moot problem, you might end up drafting something that looks a little like *Huggins v Hobdell*, the specimen moot problem contained in Appendix X. That problem also includes a ground of appeal based on the Human Rights Act 1998. This legislation played no part in *Hunter*, but it is often a useful source of grounds of appeal when drafting moot problems.

## Summary

12–59    A well organised mooting competition will attract and motivate contestants and judges alike. It will also bring "repeat business" in that spectators will return as mooters, mooters will return as judges, and judges will return as themselves.

This chapter has identified the principal elements involved in organising a successful mooting competition. They include the following:

- Devising an appropriate structure for a mooting competition.

- Obtaining sponsorship for and publicising a mooting competition.

- Recruiting and briefing judges.

- Planning and running mooting masterclasses.

- Managing the "front of house" at moots.

- Selecting and writing moot problems.

---

[6] [1997] AC 655.

# Appendices

# APPENDIX I
## LEADING INTERVARSITY COMPETITIONS

A1–1

| Jurisdiction | Name of competition | Organiser's contact details |
|---|---|---|
| England and Wales | The English-Speaking Union/Essex Court Chambers National Mooting Competition | *Vivienne_Thomson@esu.org*<br>0207 529 1550 |
| England and Wales | OUP National Mooting Competition | *Mooting.uk@oup.com*<br>0208 503 5513 |
| England and Wales | The *Weekly Law Reports* Mooting Competition | *DanC@iclr.co.uk*<br>0207 242 6471 |
| Scotland | The Alexander Stone Scottish Intervarsity Moot Court Competition | *M.Godfrey@law.gla.ac.uk* |
| International | The Philip C Jessup International Law Moot Court Competition | *Zoe.bosomworth*<br>*@jessupuk.com* |

# APPENDIX II
## FORMAT OF "KNOCKOUT" COMPETITION

The diagram below is based on a competition involving 16 teams of mooters (Teams 1–16).  **A2–1**

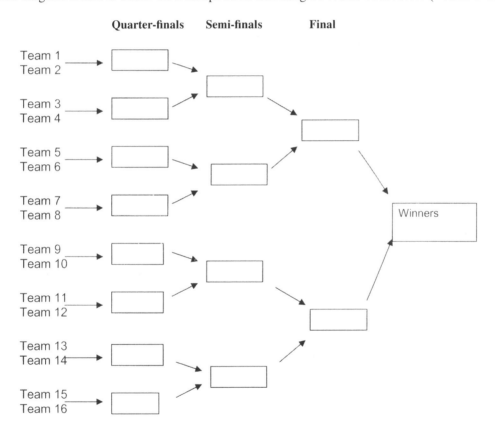

# APPENDIX III
## FORMAT OF "CHAMPIONS LEAGUE" COMPETITIONS

**A3–1**  The format described below is based on eight groups of teams (groups A-H), each containing four teams of mooters (Teams 1–4).

**Round 1**

In each group:    Team 1 v Team 2
                  Team 3 v Team 4

**Round 2**

In each group:    Team 1 v Team 3
                  Team 2 v Team 4

**Round 3**

In each group:    Team 1 v Team 4
                  Team 2 v Team 3

### "Knockout" rounds

At the end of round 3, the winners of each group (i.e. the teams with the greatest number of wins or, in the case of two- or three-way ties, the winners of any "moot-off") go into the following "knockout" rounds:

| Quarter-final | Semi-final | Final |
|---|---|---|
| Winners of group A | | |
| v | Winners of QF 1 | |
| Winners of group B | | |
| | v | Winners SF 1 |
| Winners of group C | | |
| v | Winners of QF 2 | |
| Winners of group D | | |
| | | v          Winners |
| Winners of group E | | |
| v | Winners of QF 3 | |
| Winners of group F | | |
| | v | Winners SF 2 |
| Winners of group G | | |
| v | Winners of QF 4 | |
| Winners of group H | | |

# APPENDIX IV
## SPECIMEN MOOTING COMPETITION RULES

These specimen rules contain a number of optional provisions that have been inserted in **A4–1** square brackets.

### RULES OF [INSERT INSTITUTION] MOOTING COMPETITION [2007/2008]

1.  In these Rules, the "Organiser" is defined as [insert name of organiser] or his designated representative.

2.  The competition shall be open to teams of two students both of whom shall be studying the [insert name of course] as of [insert date].

3.  [The Organiser will hold a draw to determine the members of each team. Once drawn, team members may not be changed from round to round except with the express written permission of the Organiser, which will only be given in exceptional circumstances.]

4.  The competition shall be run on a ["knockout"/"Champions League"] basis with each round taking place on the date advertised in the mooting brochure, copies of which are available from the Organiser.

5.  A moot may only be rescheduled with the express permission of the Organiser, which shall only be given in exceptional circumstances.

6.  The Organiser will hold a draw to determine the teams that will compete against each other at each moot.

7.  Each moot will have one judge except for the final of the competition, which will be presided over by three judges.

8.  The Organiser will distribute the moot problem for each round to all mooters involved by e-mail two weeks before the round is due to take place. At the same time, the Organiser will advise each team whether it represents the [appellant/reclaimer] or the respondent.

9.  The Organiser will keep a chart on his or her office door showing the progress of the competition and the result of each moot.

10. Any apparent ambiguity arising out of a moot problem shall be brought to the attention of the Organiser within three days of receipt of the problem by the teams in accordance with rule 8 above. The Organiser shall have absolute discretion to resolve the ambiguity.

11. Each team will be entitled to rely at the moot on a maximum of three authorities, i.e. reported cases, institutional writers, textbooks and journal articles. Extracts from authorities contained in any authority relied on by a team shall not constitute additional authorities for these purposes. By no later than 5pm two working days before the moot is scheduled to take place, each team must supply to the other team and to the Organiser a written list of the authorities on which it will rely at the moot.

12. [Each team must prepare a skeleton argument, which should not exceed two sheets of A4 paper, that sets out the main points of its argument and includes citations and page references for each authority on which it relies. By no later than 5pm two working days before the moot is scheduled to take place, each team will supply a copy of its skeleton argument to the other team and to the Organiser by e-mail. The judge may at his or her absolute discretion refuse to hear an argument that has not been raised in outline in a team's skeleton argument or may take the omission from the skeleton argument into account in deciding which team should win the moot.]

13. Each moot will start promptly at the starting time advised by the Organiser. If any contestant is late, the judge may decide in his or her absolute discretion to start the moot in the contestant's absence and take lateness into account in deciding which team should win the moot.

14. [At the start of the moot, each team must provide the judge with a bundle containing full unmarked photocopies or print-offs of each authority on which it will rely at the moot.]

15. Each participant shall be permitted to speak at the moot for a maximum of 10 minutes [, save that the team representing the appellant will be allowed an additional five minutes in which to reply to the respondent's case]. Time taken up in making and responding to judicial interventions will not count towards these time limits.

16. The order of speeches at the moot will be as follows: [in England and Wales—leading counsel for the appellant, junior counsel for the appellant, leading counsel for the respondent, junior counsel for the respondent and leading counsel for the appellant in reply; in Scotland—junior counsel for the appellant/reclaimer, junior counsel for the respondent, senior counsel for the appellant/reclaimer and senior counsel for the respondent].

17. At the end of the moot, the judge shall give judgment as follows: (1) an adjudication on the points of law raised in the moot and (2) a decision as to which team has won the moot, including any feedback on the participants' performances. In reaching a decision as to which team has won the moot, the judge shall take into account each of the overriding, general and specific criteria listed below.

18. There shall be no appeal against the judge's judgment.

19. Any objection to the outcome of a moot, which may only be based on an alleged infringement of these Rules, shall be made to the Organiser in writing by no later than 5pm on the day following the moot. The Organiser's decision on the objection will be final.

20. The Organiser shall have absolute discretion to amend these Rules and to resolve any question concerning their interpretation.

# CRITERIA FOR DETERMINING THE WINNER OF EACH MOOT

The criteria set out below are accompanied, where appropriate, by explanatory notes in italics.

## Overriding Criterion

- Be persuasive.

The judge will allocate approximately 10% of the overall marks to this criterion.

## General Criteria

- Speak at appropriate pace and volume.
- Be concise and use plain English.
- Structure submissions in a logical manner.
- Demonstrate appropriate manners and etiquette.

  *Mooters must be courteous to judges and opponents alike, and ensure that they are correctly attired for a moot courtroom.*

- Deal effectively with judicial interventions.
- Work as a team.
- Abide by the rules of the competition.

  *Mooters should bear in mind, in particular, the obligations to exchange lists of authorities [and skeleton arguments] timeously and to keep their submissions within the time limits allowed.*

The judge will allocate approximately 40% of the overall marks to these criteria.

## Specific Criteria

- Effectively outline the issue/s and how you propose to deal with them.
- Introduce and use authorities effectively, distinguishing where necessary.

  *Mooters should explain how each authority relates to the submission being made, ask whether the judge has read the authority and make it clear which passages are relied on.*

- [Refer to and expand upon the arguments put forward in your skeleton argument.

  *Mooters are not allowed to run arguments that are not identified in their skeleton argument.*]

- Make effective submissions that support your case.
- Accurately apply the law to the facts set out in the moot problem.
- Respond to and undermine your opponents' arguments.

The judge will allocate approximately 50% of the overall marks to these criteria.

# APPENDIX V
## SPECIMEN JUDGE'S SCORE SHEET

A5–1 The score sheet set out below is based on the criteria that appear in the specimen mooting competition rules at Appendix IV.

**Appellant**

| Name of mooter | Overriding criterion (10%) | General criteria (40%) | Specific criteria (50%) | Total | Comments |
|---|---|---|---|---|---|
| | | | | | |
| | | | | | |
| Overall team score | | | | | |

**Respondent**

| Name of mooter | Overriding criterion (10%) | General criteria (40%) | Specific criteria (50%) | Total | Comments |
|---|---|---|---|---|---|
| | | | | | |
| | | | | | |
| Overall team score | | | | | |

A6–1

[Institution] Mooting Competition [2007/08]

# Persuade me.

To find out more, contact [details]

# APPENDIX VII
## SAMPLE TEXT FOR FRESHERS' FAIR BROCHURE

**A7–1  THE [INSERT NAME OF INSTITUTION] MOOTING COMPETITION [2007/2008]**

This brochure gives a brief description of what a moot is and when the competition will take place. If you are interested in taking part, you will need to attend the introductory lecture on [insert date], at which more details will be provided.

**What is a moot?**

A moot is a form of legal argument. Two teams, each comprised of two students, are presented with a hypothetical legal problem. Each team must argue one side of the case before a judge or panel of judges. Both team members are obliged to speak, although it is up to them how they divide up the task. At the conclusion of the moot, the judge(s) will deliver judgment on the legal issues and decide which team has won the moot.

**An example of a moot**

The moot problem might describe a situation like this: party A bought goods from party B and has sued party B for damages because, A alleges, the goods were not of satisfactory quality; party A succeeded in its claim in front of the first instance court and party B is appealing against this decision on the basis that the loss is too remote. In this scenario, one team of mooters would act for party B (the appellant) and argue that the loss is too remote. The other team would act for party A (the respondent) and argue that the loss is not too remote. In order to construct their arguments, both teams would need to research the law on damages and remoteness, and look up any relevant legal authorities.

**Competition dates**

Out of fairness to all participants, every moot in any given round of the competition will take place on the same night. The dates for each round of moots are as follows:

Round one: [insert date and time]

Quarter-finals: [insert date and time]

Semi-finals: [insert date and time]

Final: [insert date and time]

Each moot will last for approximately one hour and refreshments will be available afterwards.

**The sponsor**

The competition is sponsored by [insert name of the sponsor], who have kindly provided a prize of [describe prize] to the winning team. The sponsor will also provide judges for the semi-finals and final, and will lead a mooting masterclass on [insert date].

**Next steps**

If you are interested in taking part in the competition, please give your name to [insert the name of the organiser]. You can contact him by e-mail at [insert e-mail address].

PLEASE NOTE THAT WE ARE UNABLE TO ACCOMMODATE MORE THAN 64 ENTRANTS (32 TEAMS OF 2). IN THE EVENT THAT MORE THAN 64 PEOPLE EXPRESS INTEREST, NAMES WILL BE PULLED OUT OF A HAT TO DETERMINE WHO TAKES PART. IF YOU APPLY AND ARE UNSUCCESSFUL, YOU SHOULD BE AWARE THAT AD HOC MOOTS WILL BE ARRANGED SO THAT YOU HAVE AN OPPORTUNITY TO MOOT DURING THE ACADEMIC YEAR.

# APPENDIX VIII
## SPECIMEN POST–LAUNCH POSTER

A8–1

[Institution] Mooting Competition
The Quarter-Finals
Date
Time
Sponsored by [name of firm/set of chambers]

So near, and yet so far. . .

[Names of participants]

# APPENDIX IX
## SAMPLE TEXT FOR JUDGE'S GUIDANCE NOTE

GUIDANCE NOTE FOR [INSERT INSTITUTION] MOOTING COMPETITION A9–1
[2007/2008]

1.  The organiser of the competition is [insert name]. At least one week before the moot that you will be judging, [he/she] will advise you of the venue of the moot and will provide you with a copy of the moot problem and a schedule containing the names of the mooters who will be speaking. Please take time to read the moot problem in advance of the moot and, if possible, to think about the points that you would expect both sides to make. If you will be one of a number of judges, please try to discuss the moot problem with your fellow judges before the moot.

2.  Approximately two days before the moot takes place, the organiser will send to you copies of the participants' [skeleton arguments and] lists of authorities. Please endeavour to read them before the moot.

3.  Unless you are told otherwise by the organiser, the moot will start promptly at 5.30pm. If this is going to be a problem for you, please let the organiser know as soon as possible.

4.  You are responsible for ensuring that the lay-out of the moot courtroom is to your satisfaction. Please therefore try to arrive at least 10 minutes early so that adjustments can be made to the room's lay-out if necessary.

5.  Each participant is allowed a maximum of 10 minutes in which to make oral submissions. That period does not include time spent dealing with your questions. Please do your best to ensure that the participants keep to this time limit. You might, for example, give a short warning if $10\frac{1}{2}$ minutes elapse and then refuse to hear anything further at the 11–minute mark. Whatever method you choose to adopt, please employ it consistently.

6.  You are encouraged to make interventions where appropriate during each participant's speech. So far as possible, each participant should be subjected to interventions of similar length and complexity. When asking questions of the participants, please try to test the validity of the submission being made rather than the participant's wider knowledge of the law. If a participant is visibly struggling to answer a question, please encourage him or her to move on to another point.

7.  After the participants have completed their oral submissions, the organiser will invite you to retire to another room to consider your decision. Please keep your deliberations relatively brief as we do try to complete each moot within an hour.

8.  You are asked to give a short reasoned judgment on the legal issues raised by the moot problem before announcing which team has won the moot. Either before or after giving your decision on the moot, you should briefly provide feedback on the strengths and weaknesses of each participant's performance. When you give feedback, please try to follow these short guidelines:

    (1)  focus on a small number of points, perhaps two or three, that will make the greatest difference to the overall standard of the participant's performance;

    (2)  begin your feedback by mentioning something that the participant did well; and

    (3)  when providing negative feedback, try to give concrete examples and suggest how the mistakes could have been avoided.

9.  In deciding which team has won the moot, you must have regard to the criteria set out in the competition rules, a copy of which is provided with this guidance note. Of course, these criteria can never be exhaustive and you will inevitably find yourself making some subjective judgments.

10.  There will be refreshments after the moot to which you, the participants and the audience are invited. If a participant asks you for further feedback at this point, by all means give it, but do not feel that you have to justify your decision.

11.  If you have any questions, whether prior to the moot or on the night itself, please do not hesitate to contact the organiser at [insert contact details].

# APPENDIX X
## SPECIMEN MOOT PROBLEM:
### *HUGGINS v HOBDELL*

IN THE COURT OF APPEAL (CIVIL DIVISION)

### DANIEL AND SARAH HUGGINS

-and-

### JEFFREY HOBDELL

Daniel and Sarah Huggins, who are brother and sister and both in their 20s, live in their parents' house, 78 Onslow Gardens, London N10 ("the Property"). Their parents own the Property jointly. At all material times, the parents have lived and worked in Saudi Arabia, only returning to the Property for a week each Christmas.

Jeffrey Hobdell recently bought and moved into the next-door property, 80 Onslow Gardens. Jeffrey is a member of a pagan cult that worships the sun. This involves him meeting with as many as 10 other followers of the cult in his garden at sunrise every day and marking the sunrise with a 30–minute service that consists of chanting and letting off fireworks.

Daniel and Sarah Huggins find that this ceremony interrupts their sleep, particularly in the summer. After making a series of complaints to Mr Hobdell, they commenced proceedings in the High Court alleging that the cult's activities constitute a private nuisance. They sought an injunction to restrain Mr Hobdell from engaging in chanting or from letting off fireworks. At trial, Mr Justice Rymer made the following findings of fact:

1. Both the fireworks and the chanting were clearly audible from the Huggins's bedrooms notwithstanding that the windows were double-glazed.

2. The Hugginses were in no physical danger from the fireworks.

3. Paganism did not require Mr Hobdell to chant or let off fireworks because it prescribes no single method of celebrating sunrise, but merely requires "worship of the sun and moon".

4. Mr Hobdell's sole motivation for his behaviour was his pagan belief that the sunrise should be marked.

Mr Justice Rymer refused the injunction on the following grounds:

1. Since the Hugginses had no proprietary interest in the Property, being bare licensees, they had no legal right to bring a claim for private nuisance.

2. Neither chanting nor letting off fireworks constituted an act of nuisance in this context.

3. Even if the Hugginses had a claim in private nuisance, it was subject to Mr Hobdell's right under Article 9 of the European Convention on Human Rights ("the ECHR") to manifest his religion or beliefs.

Daniel and Sarah Huggins appeal to the Court of Appeal on the following grounds:

1. That Mr Justice Rymer erred in law in finding that it is necessary to have a proprietary interest in property in order to found a claim in private nuisance.

2. That Mr Justice Rymer erred in law in finding that Article 9 of the ECHR applies in circumstances where Mr Hobdell's actions were not required by but simply motivated by his religious beliefs.

# APPENDIX XI
## SPECIMEN MOOT PROBLEM:
## *SMITH v DESIGNER FASHIONS LIMITED*

JOE SMITH

-and-

DESIGNER FASHIONS LIMITED

On 1 January 2007, Designer Fashions Limited published an advertisement in the Watford Gazette stating as follows:

> "*Want to look sharp in 2007? Then take advantage of this amazing bargain. The first man into our Watford shop on 2 January 2007 gets to buy the Armani suit of his choice for just £10.*"

Joe Smith saw the advertisement and queued up all night outside Designer Fashions' Watford shop. At 9.15am on 2 January 2007, he was the first customer admitted to the store. He selected a three-button sky blue Armani suit and proceeded to the cash desk. The sales assistant refused to sell the suit to Mr Smith for £10 stating that the promotion was no longer valid because a four-button jet black Armani suit had already been sold to the store's assistant manager, who had entered via a staff entrance at 9.00am.

Mr Smith sued Designer Fashions Limited in the Watford County Court. At first instance, Circuit Judge Pearl held that the advertisement was an invitation to treat rather than a contractual offer. She accordingly found in favour of Designer Fashions Limited and dismissed the claim.

Mr Smith appeals to the Court of Appeal on the following grounds:

1. That the learned judge erred in law in concluding that the advertisement was an invitation to treat and not an offer.

2. That the offer contained an implied term that it was only open to bona fide customers and not to staff who worked at the Designer Fashions store.

# Index

This index has been prepared using Sweet and Maxwell's Legal Taxonomy. Main index entries conform to keywords provided by the Legal Taxonomy except where references to specific documents or non-standard terms (denoted by quotation marks) have been included. These keywords provide a means of identifying similar concepts in other Sweet & Maxwell publications and online services to which keywords from the Legal Taxonomy have been applied. Readers may find some minor differences between terms used in the text and those which appear in the index. Suggestions to *taxonomy@sweetandmaxwell.co.uk*.